EDI
& G[_____]

CONTENTS

Published by Thomas Cook Publishing
The Thomas Cook Group Ltd
PO Box 227, Thorpe Wood
Peterborough PE3 6PU
United Kingdom

Telephone: 01733 503571
E-mail: books@thomascook.com

Text: © The Thomas Cook Group Ltd 2000
Maps: © The Thomas Cook Group Ltd 2000
Transport map: © TCS

ISBN 1 841570 68 0

Distributed in the United States of America by the Globe Pequot Press,
PO Box 480, Guilford, Connecticut 06437, USA.

Distributed in Canada by Whitecap Books, 351 Lynn Avenue,
North Vancouver, British Columbia, Canada V7J 2C4.

Distributed in Australia and New Zealand by Peribo Pty Limited,
58 Beaumont Road, Mt Kuring-Gai, NSW, 2080, Australia.

Publisher: Stephen York
Commissioning Editor: Deborah Parker
Map Editor: Bernard Horton

Series Editor: Christopher Catling

Written and researched by: Rebecca Ford

Cover photograph: Neil Setchfield

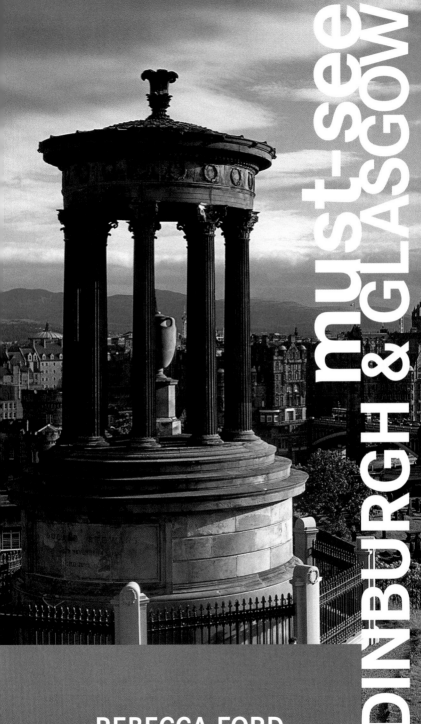

must-see
EDINBURGH & GLASGOW

REBECCA FORD

Getting to know Edinburgh & Glasgow

Discovering Edinburgh and Glasgow

The enduring image of Scotland may be a romantic mix of kilts, tartan, bagpipes and shortbread, but don't be fooled into thinking that the locals are still plucking out the heather from behind their ears. Scotland may have a rich and fascinating history but it is also a modern country, and never can it have been as confident and forward-looking as it is today. The opening of the new Scottish Parliament *seems to have filled the country with a wave of energy and optimism – and nowhere is that felt more strongly than in the cities of Glasgow and Edinburgh.*

A Tale of Two Cities

They may be only 64km (40 miles) apart, but Glasgow and Edinburgh could not be more different. **Edinburgh**, the capital and home of the new Parliament, has an ancient and dramatic history, symbolised by its magnificent castle. It is generally perceived as beautiful but slightly staid – except during the **Edinburgh Festival**, when, like an elderly maiden aunt loosening its stays, it shows the world how to party.

In contrast, **Glasgow**, Scotland's largest city, only began to grow in the 11th century. It is essentially a Victorian industrial city that flourished in the 19th century, becoming the second city of the British Empire. Unlike Edinburgh people, whose origins are Pictish, Saxon and Norman, Glaswegians have an Irish-Celtic background. For many years Glasgow suffered badly from a negative image as a run-down, violent place, full of slums such as the Gorbals. But with typical resourcefulness it has cleaned itself up (literally and metaphorically) and set about showing the world what a lot it has to offer.

There is intense rivalry between the two cities – perhaps inevitably – because they are so different. People in Edinburgh tend to speak of Glaswegians as being brash and rather common, while Glaswegians see those in Edinburgh as snobbish and unfriendly. In 1999 an article in Edinburgh's *Evening News* said that the rivalry was best summed up in Glasgow's famous and very successful advertising slogan, 'Glasgow's miles better', and the mocking response 'Edinburgh's slightly superior'. Glasgow often feels that 'Edinburgh gets everything'. There was much controversy when it was decided to berth the former Royal Yacht Britannia in Leith (with which it had no connection) instead of the Clyde (where it was built).

It is probably this very rivalry, however, that helps to make each city so vibrant. Neither is allowed to rest on its laurels for very long. Both cities have much to offer the visitor, with excellent museums and galleries, historic buildings, great shopping, flourishing arts and stylish bars and restaurants – all surrounded by stunning countryside. Getting there is easy, as they both have good air, rail and road links. And while Glasgow and Edinburgh may be very different, they are both proudly Scottish. So make sure you don't mistakenly refer to England when you mean Britain. You won't be popular.

Life in Edinburgh and Glasgow

Morning

While visitors are still tucked up in bed, a dedicated bunch of people get up and head for the swimming pools, gyms or city streets to start the day with a **burst of exercise**.

By 0800, when sightseers are just beginning to decide whether they should opt for the full Scottish breakfast or just have some tea and toast, thousands of commuters are making their way into work. Many go by car – despite severe parking difficulties. Others take trains and buses, cycle, or simply walk. Several still seem half asleep – particularly on winter mornings when it may not really get light until after 0900.

When the rush is over, visitors make for the cities' museums and galleries, or set off for a spot of retail therapy in the shops.

Afternoon

At lunchtime bars, restaurants, pubs and bistros get busy serving sandwiches and light meals. The days of long business – or liquid – lunches are gone and few people like

to eat anything too heavy during the day. Office workers frequently nip out to their favourite sandwich bar, then head back to work and eat at their desks. On sunny days in summer, every patch of green space, and every park bench, will be filled with locals frantically soaking up the sun's rays – generally muttering something like 'This may be all we're getting. Better make the most of it'.

> *Give me but one hour of Scotland, Let me see it ere I die.*
>
> **William E Aytoun, 19th-century Scottish poet and humorist**

After lunch the workers head back to their offices, and visitors get back to the serious business of shopping and sightseeing – or just settle down in a cosy café and read for an hour or two. Those who haven't eaten too much at lunchtime can go for a walk in one of the many parks and gardens.

During the summer, particularly in Edinburgh, your every move will appear to be serenaded by the busking, kilted pipers who haunt the city streets. Some are very good – others very loud.

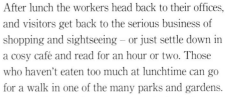

Evening

At around 1730, people begin to pour out of work and make their way back home. Some may go for a drink with friends first, others may head for the gym (generally those who can't face exercising first thing in the morning). Although winter nights are long and dark (it gets dark around 1600), summer nights seem to go on for ever and people often head off into the surrounding countryside for a walk or a drink.

Both Glasgow and Edinburgh have lively cultural scenes, and locals make the most of the fact that they have excellent drama, ballet, film, opera and music on their doorsteps. After 2000, the restaurants fill up as couples and groups of friends go out for dinner. Eating out has become so popular that there are some places where it is difficult to get a table even in the early part of the week. From around 2230 onwards the club scene gets going and the post-theatre crowd go for drinks or head home.

> *It is more astonishing than an Eastern dream. A city rises up before you painted by fire on night.*
>
> **Alexander Smith on Edinburgh at night**

Yesterday and tomorrow

Edinburgh's history stretches back thousands of years to the day when Iron-Age man first took refuge on the volcanic outcrop that we now know as Castle Rock. The defensive advantages to settling on these lonely crags are obvious and it is no wonder that by the 1st century AD*, there appears to have been a permanent stronghold on the site of the present castle.* Din Eidyn*, as the fort was known, was said to have been occupied by the Gododdin tribe.*

Edinburgh was often devastated by war and the castle besieged many times. In 1544 **Henry VIII**, determined that

the infant **Mary, Queen of Scots** should marry his son Edward, sent troops to sack the castle – an action known as the 'Rough Wooing'. Mary was sent to France for safety. The city is full of history. It was here that **John Knox** launched and led the **Scottish Reformation**, and where Mary, Queen of Scots' secretary **David Rizzio** was murdered. In 1707 the **Act of Union** with England was signed. This was so unpopular with the people that the signing had to take place in secret, probably in an Edinburgh cellar, so as to escape the attentions of the mob outside.

In the 18th century, the wall constraining the medieval Old Town was taken down, and the elegant Georgian New Town was laid out. Edinburgh became a hub of intellectual activity, a city where philosophers, physicians, writers and artists could flourish.

The writer A A Gill once described Edinburgh as 'the most perfect European city … as if designed by enlightened angels'.

Glasgow's history is far less turbulent. Founded by St Mungo in the 6th century, for hundreds of years it was an ecclesiastical city. Its university was established in 1451. Glasgow remained small until the 18th century, when trade in tobacco, rum and sugar brought wealth to the city's merchants. But it was not until the Victorian Age that Glasgow really mushroomed. Industrialisation transformed the city, as factories and engineering works opened, and the population exploded. The city was energised and great figures of the Victorian era emerged, including the physicist Lord Kelvin, who proposed the Kelvin (Absolute) temperature scale, and the surgeon Joseph Lister of the Royal Infirmary, who pioneered the use of carbolic acid as an antiseptic.

These days it is hard to keep pace with the changes taking place in Glasgow and Edinburgh. New hotels, stylish bars and innovative visitor attractions are opening all the time. Change was symbolised in 1996, when the Stone of Destiny was transferred from Westminster Abbey to Edinburgh Castle, and became inevitable after the referendum in 1997, in which the people voted 'yes' to a devolved Scottish Parliament. The Parliament opened in 1999.

Millions of pounds are now being spent on revitalising neglected parts of the two cities. A huge liner terminal and shopping complex is going up in Edinburgh's Leith. In Glasgow an area by the Clyde has been earmarked for Glasgow Harbour, an extensive development of shops, offices, homes and leisure facilities. The city will also soon boast a sparkling new Science Centre. The 21st century is here – and it could well be a golden age for these vibrant Scottish cities.

People and places

Innovators

'Mr Watson, come here, I want to see you.' This simple sentence sparked a revolution in communications, and was to affect the lives of people throughout the world. The words, spoken by Edinburgh-born Alexander Graham Bell, made up the first articulate sentence ever spoken on a telephone. Today the telephone, as well as e-mail and the Internet, are an important part of everyday life and they are all due to this inventive Scot.

Industry, inventiveness and a capacity for hard work are all qualities that Scots seem to possess in abundance. It is no wonder that so many have made their mark on the world – and their impact is often felt years after their deaths. Bell is just one example. There is also James Watt, who invented the condensing engine, apparently after a walk on Glasgow Green. His invention made the steam engine economically viable. And then there is David Livingstone, the explorer, who was born in Blantyre, outside Glasgow. Working as a medical missionary he made many journeys through Africa, his most famous discovery being the Victoria Falls. Scotland is famed for its architects too, such as Robert Adam and Charles Rennie Mackintosh.

Today one of Edinburgh's most successful entrepreneurs is Sir Tom Farmer, who opened his first tyre and car accessory business in 1964. His company, Kwik-Fit, is now of one of the world's largest car-parts repair and replacement specialists.

Writers

Edinburgh seems to have produced more than its fair share of writers. Whether they have been inspired by the city's beauty, its history or its secrets is difficult to say – perhaps it is a combination of all three. Great names from the past include Sir Walter Scott and Robert Louis Stevenson.

Oscar Wilde's **The Picture of Dorian Gray** *is said to have been based on an Edinburgh priest, Father John Gray.*

There are established authors such as Dame Muriel Spark, who once said 'Edinburgh had an effect on my mind, my prose style and my ways of thought'. Contemporary authors associated with the city include J K Rowling, who created Harry Potter, Iain Banks and Irvine Walsh.

Show-business stars

Edinburgh's most famous son is the actor Sean Connery. Born and brought up in Fountainbridge, the former James Bond once worked as a milk delivery boy. Glasgow's exuberant and outgoing nature is evident in the many famous show-business names it has produced. These include Alan Cumming, Daniella Nardini, John Hannah, Robbie Coltrane and Robert Carlyle. And of course there is Billy Connolly, the comedian and actor, who was brought up in Partick and used to work as a welder in a shipyard at Govan.

" *Edinburgh is the receptacle of culture whereas Glasgow is the generator of it.* "
Patrick Robin Archibald Boyle, 10th Earl of Glasgow

Music

Glaswegian energy is also reflected in its vibrant music scene. In the 1980s it produced bands such as Wet Wet Wet and Simple Minds. Today it has spawned Travis – apparently Noel Gallagher's favourite band – and Texas.

Getting around

General information

Glasgow – the following centres will give information on local buses, trains, the underground and ferry services, as well as tickets for coach tours, excursions and long-distance services. You can get special tickets such as a **Daytripper ticket**, which gives you unlimited travel throughout Strathclyde for one day. It allows you to travel by train, underground, most buses and some ferries.

The Travel Centre, St Enoch Square. No tel: all travel enquiries through Buchanan Bus Station (see below). Open: Mon–Sat 0830–1730.

Buchanan Bus Station, Killermont Street. Tel: (0141) 332 7133. Open: Mon–Sat 0630–2230; Sun 0700–2230.

Edinburgh
Public transport details are available from:
Traveline, 2 Cockburn Street. Tel: 0800 232323. Open Mon–Fri 0830–1630, closed weekends and public holidays.

Buses

Both Glasgow and Edinburgh have a bewildering array of buses that operate around the city centres and also to outlying areas. Edinburgh in particular is notorious for route changes, so you are advised to check with the bus company or at a travel centre before you set off.

Glasgow: one of the main bus companies is **First Glasgow**. *Tel: (0141) 423 6600.*

Edinburgh: local firms are **Lothian Buses plc** (*tel: (0131) 555 6363; open 24 hours*) and **First Edinburgh** (*tel: (0131) 663 9233*).

Tip

Make sure that you have some loose change before you get on the bus – most drivers refuse to give change.

Bus tours

Organised bus tours are a very popular way of getting to know the cities. You can take short tours showing you the main sites in the city centre, or day tours that take you further afield.

Glasgow

City tours: choose between **Guide Friday**'s open-top buses (*tel: (0141) 248 7644*) or **Discovering Glasgow Tours** (*tel: (0141) 204 0444*).

Day tours: either **Glasgow Plus** (*tel: (0141) 633 1378*) or **Cameron Tours** (*tel: (0141) 647 7283*) are recommended.

Edinburgh

Many tours operate from Edinburgh so ask at tourist information for full details.

City Tours: **Guide Friday** has open-top buses (*tel: (0131) 556 2244*).

Day Tours: **Scotline Tours** (*tel: (0131) 557 0162*).

Underground

There is no underground system in Edinburgh. Glasgow has an efficient and uncomplicated underground that follows a circular route. There is a flat fare, but you can also purchase **multi-journey tickets** from Hillhead and St Enoch travel centres. The small orange trains have given the service the nickname **'the clockwork orange'**.

Trains

Glasgow's railway stations are **Queen Street** and **Central**, Edinburgh's are **Waverley** and **Haymarket**. Trains run every 15 minutes between Glasgow Queen Street and Edinburgh Waverley during the day (half hourly on Sundays and in the evenings). You can also take trains out of town. If you'd like to travel over the famous **Forth Railway Bridge**, take a train from Edinburgh to North Queensferry in Fife. *For information on train services, ask at the station or tel: 08457 484950.*

Taxis

There are lots of taxi firms in Glasgow and Edinburgh. The main ranks for licensed taxis in Glasgow are outside **Queen Street** and **Buchanan Street** stations. The main taxi firm is **TOA** (*tel: (0141) 332 7070/332 6666*).

In Edinburgh there are taxi ranks at **Waverley** and **Haymarket** stations, and outside the **Caledonian Hotel**. Taxi firms include **Central Radio Taxis** (*tel: (0131) 229 2468*), **City Cabs** (*tel: (0131) 228 1211*) and **Radiocabs** (*tel: (0131) 225 9000*).

Driving

Traffic can be heavy in both Glasgow and Edinburgh city centres, although drivers are generally more courteous than in other major cities. Parking – especially in Edinburgh – is a nightmare and traffic wardens patrol with alarming enthusiasm. That said, hiring a car is a good idea if you want to go out of town and see some of the surrounding countryside. There are plenty of **car-hire** firms and you should be able to find details at the tourist information offices. A few names to try are:

Glasgow
Hertz Rent-a-Car;
tel: (0141) 248 7736
Avis Rent-a-Car;
tel: (0141) 221 2827
Enterprise Rent-a-Car;
tel: (0141) 221 8461

Edinburgh
Arnold Clark;
tel: (0131) 228 4747

Alexander's Car Rental;
tel: (0131) 229 3331
Century International Ltd;
tel: (0131) 455 7314.

Chauffeur tours

If you don't fancy driving but would like the convenience of a car, you could always opt for a chauffeur-driven tour. There are many companies operating in both Glasgow and Edinburgh, so ask the tourist information offices for details.

Cycling

Although more and more cycle routes are opening up, cycling in the city centre is not likely to be exactly relaxing. Once you get out of town there are some lovely cycle routes, including the Glasgow to Loch Lomond Cycleway and the Forth and Clyde and Union Canals. Ask tourist information if you are interested.

Walking

Edinburgh

Edinburgh is a small city, and although there are some steep hills, it is just made for walking. Most of the main tourist attractions are packed into a small area and, if you pick up a map at the tourist information centre (*see Practical information section*), you really shouldn't get lost. There are plenty of specialist walking tours available and these can be very good value, giving you an insight to the city and its history. Ghost tours tend to be particularly popular. Below are some of the walking companies that operate, but remember that there are plenty more:

Mercat Walking Tours;
tel: (0131) 225 6591
Auld Reekie Tours;
tel: (0131) 557 4700
Leith Walks;
tel: (0131) 555 2500

The Edinburgh Literary Pub Tour;
tel: (0131) 226 6665, 0800 328 3024
freephone for tour times
Volcano Tours;
tel: (0131) 555 5488
John Skinner;
tel: (0131) 555 3065.

Glasgow

Although Glasgow is much larger than Edinburgh, you will still be able to get to most of the main tourist sites on foot, and it is once again the best way of seeing the city. It's a hilly city, laid out on a grid system. There are a number of specialist walking tours you can take:

Alexander Thomson Society;
tel: (0141) 579 7976
Mercat Walking Tours;
tel: (0141) 772 0022
Scottish Tourist Guides Association;
tel: (01786) 447784, central
reservations 0870 6073071.

Helicopter

You wouldn't use this every day but for a real bird's-eye view of Edinburgh try Lothian Helicopters Ltd (*tel: (0131) 228 9999*).

Boat

The classic Glasgow boat trip is on the *Waverley* Paddle Steamer (*tel: (0141) 221 8152*). Generations of Glaswegians have taken the *Waverley* 'doon the watter' to destinations such as Dunoon and Arran.

Don't miss

1 Arthur's Seat, Edinburgh

One of the glories of Edinburgh is this magnificent volcanic outcrop, only a few minutes' walk from the city centre. Climb up here for wonderful views that seem to stretch for ever.
Page 27

2 The Burrell Collection, Glasgow

A showcase for the extraordinary art collection of one man, **Sir William Burrell**. Set in leafy parkland, the collection includes sculpture, tapestries and even old doorways.
Pages 136–7

3 Edinburgh Castle

Perched high on a crag, the castle is Edinburgh's most famous landmark and is steeped in Scottish history. It always looks stunning, whether shrouded in mist or bathed in the setting sun. **Pages 24–5**

4 Glasgow School of Art

This is not a museum but a prestigious art school, designed by Glasgow's most famous architect **Charles Rennie Mackintosh**. Take a student-led tour to view the interior.
Pages 90–1

5 Kelvingrove Art Gallery and Museum, Glasgow

This extravagant Victorian museum is crammed with fascinating exhibits from around the world and has an outstanding collection of paintings. It's the sort of place to which you'll want to return. **Pages 110–11**

6 The Lighthouse, Glasgow

Fresh and innovative, The Lighthouse is Scotland's **Centre for Architecture, Design and the City**. **Page 92**

7 Museums of Scotland, Edinburgh

The **Royal Museum of Scotland** and the **Museum of Scotland** are linked together, but you'll need more than one visit to get the most out of them. You will see exhibits from around the world, as well as treasures of Scotland. **Pages 30–1**

8 The New Town, Edinburgh

Only Edinburgh could have a New Town that is hundreds of years old. Wander through the streets and soak up the genteel beauty of the Georgian terraces. **Pages 38–53**

9 Palace of Holyroodhouse, Edinburgh

You don't often get to see inside a working palace. This is the Queen's official residence when she is in Scotland and history is still being made here. **Page 26**

10 The Tenement House, Glasgow

This traditional Glasgow home is almost exactly as it was when its original owner left to go into hospital. It's a real slice of social history. **Page 89**

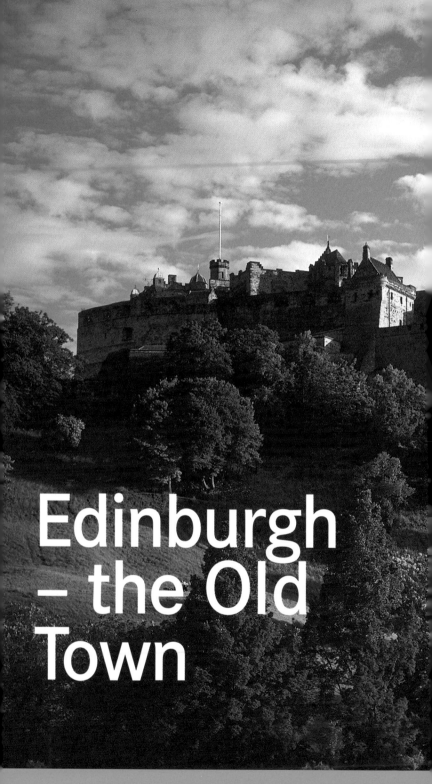

Edinburgh – the Old Town

The spirits of the past still seem to haunt Edinburgh's Old Town, which has a deliciously moody, medieval atmosphere, with tottering buildings and cobbled streets.

EDINBURGH – THE OLD TOWN

BEST OF

Edinburgh –
the Old Town

*Getting there: if you are staying in central Edinburgh you should easily be able to walk to attractions in the Old Town, which is very compact. Otherwise you can get **First Edinburgh Buses** (Nos C70, 80, 79 and 86) from Princes Street that stop along South Bridge, from where it is just a short walk. For information on **Lothian Buses**, tel: (0131) 555 6363 (open 24 hours).*

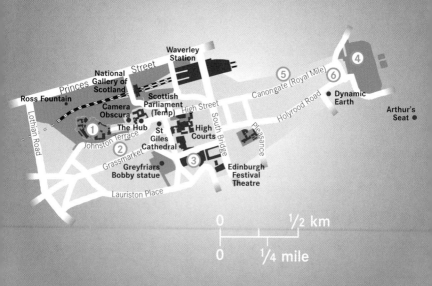

Affc
Eur

COMINGS & GOINGS

Looking for a cheap place to sleep in Europe? Check out **eurocheapo.com** for no-nonsense reviews of budget accommodations in dozens of cities. A favorite descriptive category: "the fussy aunt division" for hotels that look like a persnickety auntie decorated them. Last month, Dublin, Copenhagen, Munich, Stockholm and Berlin were added to the site bringing the lodging count up to about 600 cheapo places in Europe.... **Air France** announced that starting next year, it will take delivery of a new Airbus A-318 that is equipped with OnAir, an in-flight system that allows mobile phones to be used onboard, for flights to North Africa and within Europe.... **Austrian Airlines** is starting service from Vienna to six cities in Eastern Europe, including Yekaterinburg, Russia, and Ostrava in the Czech Republic. It is also adding flights on existing routes to several cities, including Kiev and Odessa in Ukraine, and Dubrovnik and Split in atia.... **Uptown Reservations**, a bo agency for about 80 bed-and-bre central London, is now quoti lars instead of pounds th at (800) 872-2632. Its .uptownres.co.uk pounds.... H ovated

① Edinburgh Castle

Mean, moody and magnificent, the castle is Edinburgh's crowning glory. Perched high on an extinct volcanic outcrop, it dominates the city's skyline and is understandably Scotland's number one tourist attraction.
Pages 24–5

② Grassmarket

Murders, lynchings, executions – the Grassmarket was the setting for many of the murkier events in Edinburgh's history. Today it's full of quirky shops and lively cafés, bars and restaurants.
Page 31

③ Museums of Scotland

You could easily spend a day exploring these. The Royal Museum of Scotland is an imposing Victorian building with collections that display the world to Scotland, while the new Museum of Scotland displays Scotland to the world. **Pages 30–1**

④ Palace of Holyroodhouse

Nestling at the opposite end of the Royal Mile to the Castle, Holyroodhouse is very much a working palace. The Queen's official residence in Scotland, it has strong associations with Mary, Queen of Scots. **Page 26**

⑤ The Royal Mile

Undoubtedly Edinburgh's most touristy street, the Royal Mile is also one of its most atmospheric. Once notorious for its filth, it links the Castle to the Palace of Holyroodhouse and is crammed with nooks and crannies just waiting to be explored. **Pages 28–9**

⑥ The Scottish Parliament

Scotland now has its first parliament since the 1707 Act of Union with England. It is temporarily housed near the Castle, where people have complained about Members of the Scottish Parliament (MSPs) taking cigarette breaks in the street. By 2001 the Parliament should have moved to a new building at Holyrood. **Page 27**

Tourist information
3 Princes Street. Tel: (0131) 473 3800. Open: daily.

Edinburgh Castle

Glaswegian taxi drivers love to dismiss Edinburgh as 'one street and a castle'. And although that's far from the case, the city is indisputably dominated – literally and historically – by this ancient building.

The extinct volcanic outcrop on which it is sited is of such obvious strategic importance that it is no surprise to discover that it has been a human settlement for thousands of years. *Din Eidyn*, 'the stronghold of Eidyn', appears on record by the 1st century AD and it is this that gave the city its name. The oldest part of the present castle is **St Margaret's Chapel**, built in the 12th century by **King David I**.

Over the centuries the Castle has been lost to, and recaptured from, the English many times. A reminder of its bloodthirsty

" Edinburgh is a mad god's dream. "

Hugh MacDiarmid (1892–1978)

past is Mons Meg, a giant cannon given to James II in 1457. This represented cutting-edge technology at the time and had a range of almost two miles. However, its enormous weight – more than 6 tons – made it impractical, as around 100 men were needed to haul it into battle, and it was retired from service.

Perhaps everyone's favourite exhibit in the Castle is the Honours of Scotland – the name given to the Scottish Crown Jewels. These consist of the Crown, made for James V in 1540, the Sword of State and the Sceptre. The Crown is decorated with pearls, diamonds, amethysts and garnets. After the Act of Union in 1707 the regalia was walled up in the Crown Room and only rediscovered after Sir Walter Scott received royal permission to retrieve it. They may not be as spectacular as the Crown Jewels in the Tower of London, but you can get much closer to them.

Displayed alongside the Honours is the famous Stone of Destiny, which was returned to Scotland on St Andrew's Day in 1996. One of Scotland's most powerful symbols, it was the seat on which Scottish kings were inaugurated for more than 400 years. In 1296 it was removed from Scone Abbey by Edward I and taken to England. For the next 700 years it stood in Westminster Abbey, underneath the coronation chair.

Much history has been played out in the Castle. King Charles I slept here; Oliver Cromwell made it his headquarters when his troops occupied the city and Mary, Queen of Scots gave birth to her child, James, in a room in the Royal Apartments. He was to become the King who united the Crowns of Scotland and England, as James VI of Scotland and James I of England. The Castle is also home to the Scottish National War Memorial and the one-o'clock gun, which is fired from the ramparts every day except Sunday. Originally intended to alert ships in the port of Leith, locals now use it to check their watches.

Getting there: Castle Hill. Tel: (0131) 225 1012. Open: Apr–Sept, Mon–Sun 0930–1800; Oct–Mar 0930–1700; closed 25 and 26 Dec, call for New Year opening. Last ticket sold 45 mins before closing. ££.

Palace of Holyroodhouse

Canongate, Royal Mile. Tel: (0131) 556 1096. Open: 1 Nov–31 Mar, 0930–1630 (last admission 1545); 1 Apr–31 Oct, 0930–1800 (last admission 1715). The Palace will be closed if the Queen is in residence. ££.

Holyrood has been the Royal quarter since the 12th century, when **King David I** founded an abbey here. It takes its name from a religious relic, a fragment of the **True Cross** (or 'rood') which belonged to David's mother. Scotland's kings found the Abbey more comfortable than the chilly Castle and their quarters soon grew into a palace. Most of the building you see today dates back to the reign of **Charles II** (1660–85).

The interior of the Palace is surprisingly restrained, and less opulent than many a stately home. What is fascinating is that history continues to be made here, as it serves as the **Queen's office** when she is in Scotland. The **Throne Room** is used for investitures, and during the summer garden parties are held in the grounds. The ceilings are decorated with detailed plasterwork, and the walls of the apartments hung with paintings and tapestries.

The Scottish Parliament

Opposite Holyroodhouse is the site of the new Scottish Parliament. Designed by Spanish architect Enric Miralles, the building will resemble a series of upturned boats and is due to be completed by 2001.

The most interesting rooms in the Palace are **Mary, Queen of Scots' Chambers**, which you reach by climbing a narrow, winding stairway. It was here that **David Rizzio**, her secretary, was murdered: a murder that was organised by her second husband, **Lord Darnley**. The murderers gained access to Mary's room by a secret staircase and Rizzio was stabbed 56 times. He was then dragged to an outer chamber – and guides delight in pointing out the supposedly indelible bloodstains (now accepted as fake), which colour the floor.

Arthur's Seat

This striking extinct volcano looms majestically over the Palace like a brooding giant. A walk to the top will take around twenty minutes and is well worth the effort, not just for its effective thigh-toning qualities, but also for the outstanding views it offers. They say you can even see the **Highlands** from here – on a clear day of course.

> " We sate down on a stone … overlooking a pastoral hollow as wild and solitary as any in the heart of the Highland mountains. "
>
> **Dorothy Wordsworth on climbing Arthur's Seat in 1803**

Dynamic Earth

Holyrood Road. Tel: (0131) 550 7800. Open: Easter–Oct, 1000–1800 daily; Nov–Easter, Wed–Sun 1000–1700. ££.

27

This is one for lovers of high tech and special effects. Costing over £34 million to build and looking rather like an enormous wood-louse, Dynamic Earth tells the story of the planet from the beginning of time. A lift or 'time machine' takes you down to a series of galleries, which envelop you in various periods of the earth's history. In the **Restless Earth gallery**, for instance, lava from volcanoes seems to flow towards your feet, the smell of sulphur fills the air and the ground shakes beneath you (cue lots of 'Did the earth move for you?' jokes).

The Royal Mile

Much of Scotland's history was played out along this street that runs between the Castle and Holyroodhouse. It was once notorious for its overcrowding and filth (residents would cry 'gardy-loo' before throwing the contents of their chamber pots out of the windows). After James Boswell had walked along the Royal Mile

one evening with his friend Dr Johnson, he wrote: 'I could not prevent him being assailed by the evening effluvia of Edinburgh … As we marched slowly along, he grumbled in my ear, "I smell you in the dark".'

Now the street is clean and lined with a succession of shops selling souvenirs and tartan. But it is full of interesting attractions and is highly evocative of old Edinburgh. The street is broken into four: Castlehill, Lawnmarket, High Street and Canongate.

Camera Obscura

Castlehill. Tel: (0131) 226 3709. Open: Apr–Oct, daily 1000–1800 (later in July and Aug); Nov–Mar, daily 1000–1700. ££.

The Camera Obscura, built in 1853, is like an early form of CCTV. It is essentially a giant camera with a manually operated mirror, which reflects light on to a lens and then on to a table. It is similar to watching a living, moving photograph of the city. The camera is dependent upon light, so if it is a very dull day it will not be in operation. The Camera Obscura is close to the temporary home of the Scottish Parliament.

The Hub

Castlehill. Tel: (0131) 473 2000 (ticket centre) and (0131) 473 2067 (café).
Open: winter: ticket centre Mon–Sat 0930–1700, café 0930–2300; summer:
ticket centre daily 0930–at least 1700, café 0830–2300 (much later during the
Festival). Admission varies according to ticket choice.

Opened in 1999, the Hub is the permanent home of the
Edinburgh International Festival. Built in 1840 for the
Church of Scotland, it was designed by James Gillespie
Graham and Augustus Pugin – the latter is famed for his
work on the Houses of Parliament at Westminster. Although
it is a Grade A listed building, it was practically derelict when
it was acquired by the International Festival. Now it has
been renovated, with the Gothic interiors given a snappy,
contemporary look.

St Giles' Cathedral

By George IV Bridge. Tel: (0131) 225 9442. Open: Easter–Sept, Mon–Fri
0900–1900, Sat 0900–1700, Sun 1300–1700; Oct–Easter, Mon–Sat
0900–1700, Sun 1300–1700.

Also known as the High Kirk of St Giles, this is Scotland's
main cathedral and dates back to the 12th century. With an
intense, gloomy appeal, it is the church from which John
Knox launched the Reformation in Scotland. Inside is a
plaque to Jenny Geddes who, legend has it, threw a stool
at the preacher when he attempted to introduce the English
prayer book to Scotland.

> " *Passing a Royal Mile close*
> *entrance late at night,*
> *even after gentrification,*
> *one still half expects a*
> *footpad … to step out of*
> *that dark precipitous*
> *mouth, or maybe the*
> *ghosts of Hume and Adam*
> *Smith, about to reel home*
> *after too much claret.* "
>
> **Angus Calder in**
> ***The Herald*, 1999**

Other options

Other places worth visiting
along the Royal Mile include
the Writers' Museum
(*tel: (0131) 529 4901; open:*
Mon–Sat 1000–1700); Scotch
Whisky Heritage Centre
(*tel: (0131) 220 0441; open:*
daily 0930– 1800) and Mary
King's Close (*tours led daily*
by Mercat Walking Tours; tel:
(0131) 225 6591 or (0131) 557
6464; book in advance).

Museums of Scotland

Museum of Scotland

Chambers Street. Tel: (0131) 247 4422; www.nms.ac.uk/mos/main. Open: Mon–Sat 1000–1700 (open till 2000 Tues); Sun 1200–1700. £ (price includes entry to the Royal Museum; admission is free on Tues from 1630–2000).

Opened in 1998, this new museum brings together more than 10,000 of Scotland's most precious artefacts for the first time. Housed in a cavernous modern building that is reminiscent of a Scottish baronial castle, it's the sort of place where you can easily get lost searching for a particular exhibit and end up in the toilets.

The museum covers over 3 million years of Scotland's history, from its geological formation and early peoples, to the end of the 20th century. The displays are enlivened by multimedia presentations. Some of the most important exhibits in the museum include the Hunterston brooch, made around AD 800; the Monymusk Reliquary, a tiny 8th-century shrine, which supposedly inspired Robert the Bruce's army to victory at Bannockburn in 1314; and the Lewis chess pieces, carved in the 12th century. There is also a silver travelling canteen belonging to Bonnie Prince Charlie, which was recovered after his final defeat in 1745.

Bonnie Prince Charlie was one of the names given to Prince Charles Edward Stewart (or Stuart) (1720–88), the claimant to the throne, whose troops were crushed by the Duke of Cumberland's forces at Culloden in 1746. He famously escaped to the islands dressed as the maid of Flora Macdonald. He was also known as the 'Young Pretender' and the 'Young Chevalier'. The grandson of James VII (of Scotland) and II (of England), he was born in Rome and became the focus of the Jacobite cause. After Culloden he lived in Paris and Florence and assumed the title of Charles III of Great Britain. He died in Rome and was buried at Frascati, later St Peter's.

Don't miss less well-known but nevertheless fascinating exhibits. One of these is a collection of miniature coffins discovered by accident on Arthur's Seat. Several contain a small, carved figure. They have never been explained, although some think

> *The outsides of old Edinburgh churches frightened her, they were of such dark stone, like presences almost the colour of the Castle rock, and were built so warningly with their upraised fingers.*
>
> **Dame Muriel Spark, *The Prime of Miss Jean Brodie***

they were part of a mock burial for the victims of **Burke and Hare**, the body-snatchers.

On the top floor is a collection of objects nominated by Scottish people as having made a significant impact on the 20th century. They range from a tin hat, which saved a soldier's life in the First World War, to a Wonderbra and a biro.

Royal Museum of Scotland

Chambers Street. Tel: (0131) 247 4219. Admission price and opening times as for the Museum of Scotland.

This splendid traditional museum has an impressive glass-topped roof and is conveniently linked to the new Museum of Scotland. Displays cover natural history, science and technology, archaeology and the decorative arts. There are particularly fine displays of **Chinese and Japanese art**, as well as exhibits such as the **Wylam Dilly**, the world's oldest steam engine.

Greyfriars Bobby

Candlemaker Row.

This famous statue commemorates the Skye terrier who faithfully maintained a vigil over his master's grave for 14 years. He and his master are both buried in nearby Greyfriars Churchyard.

Grassmarket

The ghosts of the past haunt the Grassmarket. It was the place to which the notorious **body-snatchers** Burke and Hare lured their victims, before murdering them and selling their bodies to science. Leading from the Grassmarket is **Victoria Street**, a lovely winding street lined with quirky and individual shops.

You can also visit the **Scottish Parliament Visitor Centre**, situated on George IV Bridge until the new Parliament building is finished (*Scottish Parliament general enquiries tel: (0131) 348 5000; www.scottish-parliament.co.uk; open: Mon–Fri 0930–1700*).

Eating and drinking

The Old Town and its neighbouring streets are brimming with restaurants, cafés, bars and pubs. There is something to suit all budgets, appetites and tastes – you can eat everything from Scottish to Spanish or South African. You are advised to book a table, especially at weekends, as places can get extremely busy. During the Festival many places open extra late.

Restaurants and bistros

The Atrium
10 Cambridge Street. Tel: (0131) 228 8882. £££. One of the most hyped restaurants in Edinburgh, the Atrium specialises in quality Scottish produce, which is given a hint of the East.

Black Bo's
57–61 Blackfriars Street. Tel: (0131) 557 6136. ££. Gourmet vegetarian food that will please even the most hardened carnivore.

Bleu
36–8 Victoria Street. Tel: (0131) 226 1900. ££. Innovative French food in chic surroundings.

blue bar café
10 Cambridge Street. Tel: (0131) 221 1222. ££. Cool and classy, blue draws a stylish crowd keen to try the contemporary food, such as venison and redcurrant sausages.

The Doric Tavern
15/16 Market Street. Tel: (0131) 225 1084. ££. The Doric is an Edinburgh institution, with a loyal local following. It dishes up fresh Scottish produce and has a great choice of wines.

The Grain Store
30 Victoria Street. Tel: (0131) 225 7635. ££. There's a cosy, romantic feel to this restaurant, serving imaginative Franco-Scottish dishes.

Iguana
41 Lothian Street. Tel: (0131) 220 4288. £. Trendy bar-bistro popular with students and clubbers. Come for coffee, light dishes or breakfast.

Kalpna
2–3 St Patrick's Square. Tel: (0131) 667 9890. ££. Excellent vegetarian Indian food often described as some of the best in Britain.

Nicolson's
6a Nicolson Street. Tel: (0131) 557 4567. ££. Elegant, with imaginative food, this restaurant is conveniently situated for the Festival Theatre. It used to be a café and is where J K Rowling wrote the first Harry Potter book.

Le Sept
7 Old Fishmarket Close. Tel: (0131) 225 5428. Lively restaurant in an atmospheric location, noted for its crêpes.

The Tower
Museum of Scotland, Chambers Street. Tel: (0131) 225 3003. ££–£££. Chic interior and great views of the Castle. Dishes range from salmon fishcakes to braised pheasant.

The Witchery by the Castle
Castlehill, Royal Mile. Tel: (0131) 225 5613. £££. Once a meeting place for medieval Satanists, this is now one of the capital's most popular eateries. It's romantic, the food's great and there's an award-winning wine list.

Just south of the Old Town is Bruntsfield, which has plenty of bars and restaurants. A couple worth trying are:

Montpeliers
159–61 Bruntsfield Place. Tel: (0131) 229 3115. ££.

Howies
208 Bruntsfield Place. Tel: (0131) 221 1777. ££.

Cafés

Café Hub
Castlehill, Royal Mile. Tel: (0131) 473 2015. £–££. Sleek café serving food as well as coffee. A great place to collapse in after hitting the tourist spots on the Royal Mile.

Caffe Lucano
37–9 George IV Bridge. Tel: (0131) 225 6690. £. Creamy cappuccinos, Italian food and tasty cakes.

Elephant House
21 George IV Bridge. Tel: (0131) 220 5355. £. Comfortable café where you can settle down with the papers or restore your energy with a light meal.

Negociants
45–7 Lothian Street. Tel: (0131) 225 6313. £. A really mixed crowd mingle here. Good for light meals as well as coffees and drinks.

Pâtisserie Florentin
8 St Giles Street. Tel: (0131) 225 6267. £. Bohemian atmosphere and French pastries.

Tearoom

Clarinda's
69 Canongate. Tel: (0131) 557 1888. £. Great traditional tearoom, with pretty tablecloths and delicious home baking.

Shopping

The Old Town is a great hunting ground for those who love specialist, quirky shops.

Royal Mile

The Old Children's Bookshelf
Tel: (0131) 558 3411. Bookworms will discover a wide selection of old children's books in this charming store.

Palenque
Tel: (0131) 557 9553. Sells Mexican handmade jewellery.

R Somerville
Tel: (0131) 556 5225. Stocks the largest selection of playing and tarot cards in the world.

Grassmarket and Victoria Street

Where to start? Antiques, books, clothes, jewellery, brushes and lace – they all abound here.

Armstrongs
Tel: (0131) 220 5557. An Aladdin's cave stuffed with vintage clothing.

The Cooks Bookshop
Tel: (0131) 226 4445. Budding chefs can revel in cookery books galore. This gourmet's delight is owned by 'one fat lady', Clarissa Dickson Wright.

Ian Mellis
Tel: (0131) 226 6215. Scrummy cheese shop.

George IV Bridge

Illumini
Tel: (0131) 556 3292. Take time to pop in and marvel at the gorgeous handmade stained glass, and Tiffany-style lamps.

Victoria Street ☞

EDINBURGH – THE OLD TOWN

City festivals

Every August, Edinburgh buzzes with vitality as the capital is taken over by the Edinburgh International Festival, *the largest cultural event of its kind in the world. The Festival started in 1947, as a symbolic post-war gesture of international co-operation. Its reputation grew quickly and it was able to attract the very best writers, musicians and performers. Over the years, artists of the calibre of* Yehudi Menuhin, Maria Callas, Placido Domingo, Rudolph Nureyev *and* Ian McKellan *have performed here.*

With the Festival came **the Fringe**, created in 1947 when six performers, put out at not having been invited to the Festival, decided to turn up anyway. The Fringe guarantees nothing – except the unexpected. None of the acts is vetted or invited to take part; performers tend to use unusual theatre spaces, and they take their own financial risks. This gives it an extraordinary vitality. Cafés, bars and tiny rooms become Fringe venues and Edinburgh's streets fill with fire-eaters, mime artists and stilt walkers. Shows in the past have ranged from a dog that hypnotised the audience to an erotic trapeze act featuring fresh fruit. Sharp comedy acts compete for the prestigious **Perrier Award**, and much of the city stays open twenty-four hours a day. Many great names have emerged from the Fringe, including **Alan Bennett**, **John Cleese**, **Maggie Smith**, **Derek Jacobi**, **Emma Thompson** and **Stephen Fry**.

Several other festivals also take place in August. There's the **Jazz Festival**, the **Military Tattoo**, the **Film Festival** (of

Vogue *once described the Edinburgh Film Festival as 'the hippest gathering for cineastes'.*

which John Huston once said 'it's the only film festival that's worth a damn') and the Book Festival. Acclaimed authors appearing at recent Book Festivals have included Doris Lessing, Peter Ackroyd and Beryl Bainbridge. Every year events conclude with a spectacular firework display from Edinburgh Castle.

Although the Edinburgh Festival is the big one, Glasgow hosts an annual Celtic Connections Festival each January, celebrating Celtic musical culture. It also has an International Jazz Festival, which has attracted artists such as Nina Simone. Both cities also pride themselves on their Hogmanay (New Year) celebrations, which take over the streets and go on for days.

Edinburgh – the New Town

Edinburgh's New Town is now well over 200 years old. Its airy streets and elegant Georgian squares make a striking contrast to the unruly tenements and brooding castle of the Old Town.

EDINBURGH – THE NEW TOWN

BEST OF

Edinburgh – the New Town

Getting there: you can walk to the New Town if you are staying in central Edinburgh. Otherwise you can travel on **First Edinburgh buses** *(Nos 79 and 80) from Princes Street to Charlotte Square, or buses 64 and 65 run along George Street. Tel: (0131) 555 6363 (open 24 hours) for information on services run by Lothian Buses plc.*

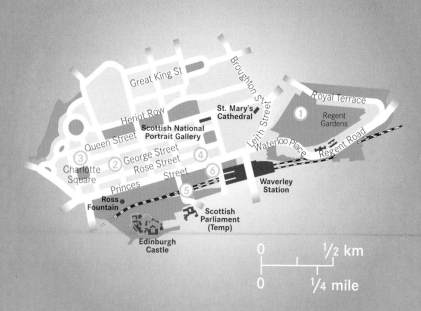

① Calton Hill

Topped with a half-finished replica of the Parthenon in Athens, Calton Hill makes an arresting sight. Climb up to the top for stunning views of the city and Arthur's Seat. **Page 46**

② George Street

It was once noted more for its sober banks and financial institutions than its social scene. Now George Street is lined with designer-clothes shops and buzzes with trendy bars and lively restaurants. **Page 48**

③ The Georgian House

Dating back to 1796, the Georgian House is a typically elegant New Town property. A visit here gives you an insight into the lives of the residents of this fashionable 18th-century development. **Page 43**

④ Jenners

This grand old department store is often described as Scotland's version of Harrods – although in reality it is more like Fortnum & Mason. Join the well-heeled ladies of Edinburgh in the hunt for perfumes, designer clothes – and shortbread. **Page 47**

⑤ National Gallery of Scotland

Discover one of the best Western art collections in Europe. Works by all the great masters such as **Turner**, **Rembrandt** and **Van Gogh**, as well as a great collection of Scottish art. **Pages 44–5**

41

⑥ Scott Monument

This grand Gothic spire is one of Edinburgh's most famous sights. It commemorates the local writer **Sir Walter Scott** and is the largest monument to an author in the world. **Page 47**

Edinburgh's New Town

People are frequently surprised when they see Edinburgh's New Town – for this is no soulless modern estate, but an elegant and extensive Georgian development.

For centuries Edinburgh was enclosed by a defensive wall, which so confined the city that people were forced to build upwards, creating the distinctive teetering tenements (or 'lands') you see today in the Old Town. After union with England, the city was freed from the danger of invasion and expanded rapidly. The Nor'Loch, a loch beneath the Castle, was drained and a bridge was constructed across the chasm. By the mid-18th century, the architect James Craig had begun work on the New Town – a planned zone of wide, airy streets, quiet squares and sweeping crescents. Wealthy inhabitants moved here in their droves, keen to escape the filth of the Old Town and it soon became the hub of 'society' in the city.

Charlotte Square

You almost feel as though you should wear your best clothes to come to Charlotte Square, designed by Robert Adam in 1791, because it ranks among the finest New Town squares. Strolling through its splendour, one can easily imagine the square peopled with the glitterati of Georgian Edinburgh. Number 6 is the official residence of the Secretary of State for Scotland and every year the gardens in the centre of the square become home to the Edinburgh Book Festival.

The Georgian House

Charlotte Square. Tel: (0131) 226 3318; www.nts.org.uk. Open: Apr–Oct, Mon–Sat 1000–1700; Sun 1400–1700. ££.

The Georgian House is a typical New Town property and gives you a vivid insight into the lives of its residents. Built in 1796, the house is now owned by the National Trust for Scotland and the interior has been restored to its original appearance.

> " *A hot bed of genius.* "
>
> **Tobias Smollett (1721–71),** *Humphry Clinker,* **on Edinburgh**

The airy drawing-room where guests would have been received is hung with paintings, including works by Alexander Naysmyth, Allan Ramsay and Jan van Goyen. The table in the dining room is laid for dinner, which would have been eaten early, at around 3 or 4 o'clock in the afternoon. Next to the dining room is a portable toilet, an imposing contraption that children find fascinating.

An elaborate four-poster bed dominates the bedroom. A portable medicine chest in one corner contains a selection of lotions and potions that would have been in general use in most houses. There is also a mighty Georgian brass syringe, which looks as though it was designed for horses, but was in fact used to administer enemas into unfortunate patients.

Alexander Graham Bell

One of Scotland's most influential exports was Alexander Graham Bell, the inventor of the telephone. Born in 1847 at 16 South Charlotte Street, by Charlotte Square, Bell was interested in speech early on. Following his graduation from Edinburgh University, the family emigrated to America. Bell became a teacher of the deaf in Boston, and his studies into the artificial reproduction of vowel sounds, using electricity and magnetism, ultimately led to the development of the telephone.

A prolific inventor, Bell also produced a wheel-shaped kite (a precursor to the helicopter), showed fishermen how to produce fresh water from sea water and designed a floating concrete dock – the same design was used in the 1944 Normandy landings. There are plans to turn Bell's birthplace into a museum dedicated to his life and work.

National Gallery of Scotland

The National Gallery of Scotland is one of those places where you can come again and again and always find a work of art to suit your mood.

It was built in the early 19th century on **The Mound** (literally a mound of earth and rubble, created by the building of the New Town) and contains a fine collection of Western art. It is particularly noted for its Italian and Scottish paintings. Works are displayed as they would have been when the gallery first opened, giving a cosy, cluttered effect. Quite a number of works are on loan from the Duke of Sutherland.

The greatest strengths of the **Italian collection** are the paintings by **Raphael**, **Titian** and **Tintoretto**. Raphael's work includes the *Holy Family with a Palm Tree* and the celebrated painting of the Virgin and Child, known as the *Bridgewater Madonna*. Among the Titians are *Diana and Actaeon* and *Diana and Callisto*, both of which were inspired by **Ovid**'s *Metamorphoses* and were painted for Philip II of Spain. There is also a delicate and moving work by **Filippino Lippi** entitled *The Nativity with Two Angels*. Later Italian works include **Giovanni Tiepolo**'s vigorous *The Finding of Moses* and **Francesco Guardi**'s *View of St Mark's, Venice*.

A small collection of Spanish paintings incorporates works by El Greco and Velázquez, and among the Flemish and Dutch works is a precious series of 15th-century altarpiece panels by Hugo van der Goes. They were commissioned for a Scottish church by its provost Edward Bonkil, who is depicted in one of the panels.

Among the sculptures owned by the museum is Canova's famous *The Three Graces*, representing the three daughters of Jupiter and Eurynome. The work was acquired at great expense – and amid some controversy – with assistance from various bodies including John Paul Getty II. It is owned jointly with the Victoria and Albert Museum in London and spends some seven years or so at each location. It will next be in Edinburgh around 2005.

> " ... inside it was very grand in an imperial, nineteenth-century sort of way ... it rather brought to mind a stroll through Queen Victoria's boudoir. "
>
> **Bill Bryson on the Scottish National Gallery, *Notes from a Small Island***

Landscape paintings include Claude Lorrain's *Landscape with Apollo and the Muses*. His idealised, picturesque works were once so fashionable that people used to admire natural landscapes through a coloured disc of glass, known as a 'Claude glass'. Claude heavily influenced John Constable whose famous *Dedham Vale* is also in the gallery. Additionally there are landscapes by Cuyp, Pissarro and Monet. Every January the gallery mounts a fine display of around 30 works by Turner. The paintings were acquired through an odd bequest, which firmly stipulated that they should only be exhibited in January, as light levels are lower and the paintings would be less likely to be damaged.

The gallery's most important recent acquisition is Botticelli's *The Virgin adoring the sleeping Christ Child*. The painting formerly belonged to the Earl of Wemyss and was destined for the Kimbell Museum in Texas before a frantic fund-raising effort secured the painting for the gallery – at a price tag of £10 million.

Getting there: The Mound. Tel: (0131) 624 6200. Open: Mon–Sat 1000–1700; Sun 1400–1700. Admission free; charges for special exhibitions.

Princes Street

This wide, spacious avenue marks the edge of the New Town. It is lined on one side by shops and on the other by Princes Street Gardens, attractive communal gardens created on the site of the Nor'Loch. Although it is no longer Scotland's finest shopping street, it is always extremely busy and a favourite haunt of tartan-clad pipers, busking during the Festival.

Calton Hill

A volcanic outcrop, Calton Hill dominates the eastern end of Princes Street and is topped with an extraordinary variety of Grecian-style monuments, erected in the 19th century. There is the Grecian-domed City Observatory; the Nelson Monument (*tel: (0131) 556 2716; £*), completed in 1807 to celebrate victory at Trafalgar; the Burns Monument, styled on a Corinthian temple, and the National Monument, intended to honour the soldiers killed in the Napoleonic Wars. This was to have been a full-scale replica of the Parthenon in Athens, but funding ran out before it could be finished. You might lose a bit of puff getting up here, but the views are stunning and well worth the effort.

" *It is the place to stroll on one of those days of sunshine and east wind which are so common in our more than temperate summer.* "

Robert Louis Stevenson on Calton Hill

Jenners

Princes Street. Tel: (0131) 225 2442. Open: Mon and Wed 0900–1730; Tues 0930–1730; Thur 0900–1930; Fri and Sat 0900–1800.

Often called Scotland's **Harrods**, this famous department store is a real city institution. Founded by **Charles Jenner**, an Englishman, the store opened in 1838. Initially times were so hard that Jenner had to sleep on a mat behind the counter, but the business soon grew. It embodies Edinburgh's genteel side and is one of the few grand old buildings left on Princes Street. Its range of menswear has been praised by *FHM* magazine.

Scott Monument

East Princes Street Gardens. Tel: (0131) 529 4068. Open: Mar–May and Oct, Mon–Sat 0900–1800; June–Sept, Mon–Sat 0900–2000, Sun 1000–1800; Nov–Feb, Mon–Sat 0900–1600, Sun 1000–1600. £.

The gorgeously Gothic Scott Monument was erected by public subscription in memory of **Sir Walter Scott**, the city's most famous resident. At 61m (200ft) high, it is one of the city's most distinctive landmarks and the world's largest memorial to an author. If you're feeling fit, you can climb the 287 steps to the top.

Scottish National Portrait Gallery

1 Queen Street. Tel: (0131) 624 6200. Open: Mon–Sat 1000–1700; Sun 1400–1700. Hours extended during the Festival. Admission free; charges for special exhibitions.

Situated at the heart of the New Town, the Scottish National Portrait Gallery has been likened to a shrine. It was intended to serve as 'the highest incentive to true patriotism' and is worth seeing for the building alone. An enormous **Gothic** confection, the red sandstone exterior is studded with life-size sculptures, while the main hall is decorated with a frieze of famous Scots. The gallery displays images of famous – and infamous – Scots and the majority of works are by Scottish artists.

Portraits include **Sir Henry Raeburn**'s portrayal of Sir Walter Scott and **Alexander Naysmyth**'s well-known painting of **Robert Burns**. Look out for the photograph of

Sean Connery, taken by **Annie Leibovitz**; the ceramic by clothes designer **Jean Muir**; the painting of **Robbie Coltrane** and a cartoon of **Sir Harry Lauder**. Royalty reigns here too, from **Prince Charles Edward Stuart** to **Queen Elizabeth, The Queen Mother**. Don't miss the poignant work by **Sir Anthony Van Dyck**: painted in 1637, it depicts the little Princesses Elizabeth and Anne, two of the children of **Charles I**. Princess Anne died in 1640, aged three. Then came the English Civil War, during which

Princess Elizabeth was kept under house arrest by the Parliamentarians. She never recovered from the news of her father's execution in 1649 and died, aged 15, in 1650.

George Street

The New Town has always been the natural home of lawyers and accountants and George Street in particular was once characterised by its high proportion of banks and financial institutions. At lunchtime sober-suited men would stroll outside for a sandwich and a newspaper – and that was about as exciting as it got.

In recent years, however, George Street has been transformed. The opening of the Scottish Parliament has created a new air of confidence and energy in Edinburgh – and nowhere is it more evident than here. Market changes have caused many of the banks to close down and they have been quickly turned into trendy bars and restaurants, often with stunning interiors. Restaurants get so busy at night that one newcomer, Est Est Est, was able to turn away Mick Jagger and his party when he turned up without having booked a table. A former insurance company building is being converted into a multi-million-pound shopping mall, and many designer-clothes shops have opened up. It is now *the* place to come if you want to do some serious shopping or soak up Edinburgh's vibrant new atmosphere.

" When Edinburgh has laid her hand upon a man's shoulder, the memory of that touch does not readily fade or be easily forgot. "
Lord Cameron, address to the Edinburgh Sir Walter Scott Club, 1966

Shopping

Aside from the usual high-street chains on Princes Street, stroll along George Street and you'll be spoilt for choice with more up-market shops. Karen Millen, Jigsaw Menswear, Hobbs, Escada, Phase Eight, The Cashmere Store and Cruise have all established themselves here and many more developments are in the pipeline – including a high-class shopping mall on the corner of George Street and Castle Street.

Also on George Street are Neal's Yard Remedies, for aromatherapy oils and cosmetics, and Decorum, for designer homeware, including well-known names such as Alessi and Kosta Boda glassware. In nearby Thistle Street is Jane Davidson, selling designer clothes from Helmut Lang to Christian Dior.

Harvey Nichols has chosen Edinburgh for its second out-of-London store, which will open in 2001 in St Andrew Square.

Nightlife

Po Na Na

43b Frederick Street. Tel: (0131) 226 2224. This is a popular club/bar, attracting a slightly older, professional crowd.

Eating and drinking

There's plenty of choice in the New Town, but places do get filled up so it's best to book at weekends. If you prefer a traditional pub, head for Rose Street.

Bars and restaurants

36
36 Great King Street. Tel: (0131) 556 3636. ££. Delicious and innovative Scottish cuisine served in elegant surroundings.

All Bar One
29–31 George Street. Tel: (0131) 226 9971. £–££. Housed in the old Clydesdale Bank, this relaxed bar is a great place for coffees, drinks or meals. It's a favourite with young professionals and shoppers.

Café Royal Oyster Bar
17a West Register Street. Tel: (0131) 556 4124. ££. Dine on fish dishes, caviar and, of course, oysters, while you marvel at the grand Victorian tiled interior.

The Dome
14 George Street. Tel: (0131) 624 8624. ££. This rather glamorous restaurant is another converted bank and has a stunning glass ceiling that gives it real character. A favourite with well-heeled shoppers, it's also a good place for an evening meal.

Est Est Est
135a George Street. Tel: (0131) 225 2555. £–££. Stylish Italian restaurant, with lots of clean, blond wood, offering imaginative *antipasti* and tasty pizzas.

Henderson's Bistro
25 Thistle Street. Tel: (0131) 225 2605. £. Popular, good-value, vegetarian food. Try chestnut and red wine pâté with oatcakes, or roasted vegetable filo parcels.

Number One
1 Princes Street. Tel: (0131) 557 6727. £££. This up-market restaurant is the sort of place you treat yourself to on special occasions.

Siam Erawan
48 Howe Street. Tel: (0131) 226 3675. ££. Excellent Thai food down in the New Town. Loads of delicious dishes with delicate flavours.

Stac Polly
29–33 Dublin Street. Tel: (0131) 556 2231. ££. One of the best places to come for contemporary Scottish food, with lots of game – and the ubiquitous haggis.

Afternoon tea

The Palm Court
Balmoral Hotel, 1 Princes Street. Tel: (0131) 556 2414. ££. Revel in the sumptuous surroundings and tune into the harp tinkling in the background, while you tuck into the scones and pastries of a stylish traditional tea.

Cafés

Glass and Thompson
2 Dundas Street. Tel: (0131) 557 0909. £. Aromatic coffee, delicious cakes and deli-style snacks.

51

Edinburgh's dark secrets

Edinburgh has often been described, by Glaswegians at least, as being 'all fur coat and nae knickers' – a reference to the city's beautiful and genteel appearance, which successfully hides its darker, more lubricious nature. There is no doubt that Edinburgh has never been quite as respectable as it appears. The two faces of the city are neatly symbolised in the architectural divisions of the city centre: on the one side, the intricate, medieval web of the Old Town and, on the other, the broad streets and gracious Georgian crescents of the New Town.

It was this 'dual personality' that inspired one of the 19th century's most enduring works of fiction – *Dr Jekyll and Mr Hyde*. Robert Louis Stevenson based his character on Deacon Brodie, a 17th-century Edinburgh councillor. A model of respectability by day, he secretly had two mistresses and turned into a burglar at night. Brodie was eventually caught and hanged – on a gallows of his own design.

Even darker deeds took place in the Grassmarket, where the body-snatchers Burke and Hare lured their victims, before murdering them. They then sold the bodies to an eminent physician who used them for scientific research.

The murkier aspects of Edinburgh's past have given rise to many tales of the supernatural. The Old Town is particularly rich in ghosts, who not only haunt the dark closes of the Royal Mile, but also roam Holyroodhouse. The New Town has its stories too. Ann Street in Stockbridge was once described as 'the best haunted street in Europe'. Ghosts inhabiting its elegant houses include a Grey Lady, who engages in the alarming practice of disappearing through walls.

Perhaps Edinburgh's greatest secret is the existence of a hidden city, created to relieve over-crowding in the Old Town. Underground dwellings and streets were dug beneath the tenements, exploiting the soft sandstone ridge that led to the castle. A rabbit warren of slums developed and was occupied by the poorest in the city. You can still see a fragment of this hidden city at Mary King's Close, an ancient street deep below the City Chambers, which was inhabited until the late 19th century.

> This aristocratic, respectable old city of ours has a tradition of subterranean evil which it has not yet shaken off.
>
> **Moray McLaren,**
> *The Pursuit*

Edinburgh – the West End and Stockbridge

Georgian and Victorian buildings mingle in the West End – the last part of the New Town to be developed. Stockbridge has retained its village identity – shops here sell everything from designer goods to humble vegetables.

EDINBURGH – THE WEST END AND STOCKBRIDGE

Edinburgh – the West End and Stockbridge

*Getting there: it is not far to **walk** from the centre of town. The nearest train station to the modern art galleries is Haymarket, from where it will take 15–20 minutes to walk. **Lothian Buses** also run to the West End, Stockbridge and the Royal Botanic Garden. Tel: (0131) 555 6363 (open 24 hours).*

① The Dean Gallery

Edinburgh's newest art gallery displays the works of local-born sculptor Eduardo Paolozzi. It also has one of the most important collections of Dadaist and Surrealist works in the world. **Pages 58-9**

② Dean Village

Stroll along the Water of Leith to this ancient industrial village hidden away in a steep-sided gorge. You would never believe you were only a few minutes away from the city centre. **Page 64**

③ Royal Botanic Garden

Founded in the 17th century on an area the size of a tennis court, the Botanic Garden now covers 31 hectares and is filled with rare and beautiful plants from around the world. **Page 65**

④ Scottish National Gallery of Modern Art

The serene neo-Classical building presents a striking contrast to the lively collection of modern works of art within. Artists exhibited range from Pablo Picasso to Andy Warhol. **Pages 60-1**

⑤ St Stephen Street

There's a bohemian feel to this little street in the heart of Stockbridge. Locals love to come on Saturday afternoons and browse in the quirky shops, selling antiques, bric-a-brac and clothes. **Page 63**

⑥ Water of Leith

This river played an integral role in the development of Edinburgh as an industrial city. Now a walkway runs along its length, bringing a touch of the countryside to the heart of the city. **Pages 64-5**

57

The Dean Gallery

The West End is heaven for lovers of modern art. After you've explored the Dean Gallery, you can cross the road and investigate the Scottish National Gallery of Modern Art. The Dean Gallery is a stylish and atmospheric gallery that opened in 1999, primarily to house a large collection of works donated by Edinburgh-born sculptor, Eduardo Paolozzi.

The collection is housed in a palatial, Grade A listed building, designed in 1833 as the Dean Orphan Hospital. The managers of the orphanage commissioned it in order to escape from the increasingly unhygienic conditions in the Old Town. There was sufficient room to accommodate 200 orphans, whose daily life consisted of a strict routine of early rising, religious study, schoolwork and manual chores. The restoration of the edifice has been imaginative, with dramatic vistas and bold use of colour and light.

> " *Edinburgh's true worth lies in the revelations it affords us from unexpected quarters.* "
>
> **Financial Times**

Paolozzi is a sculptor with a distinctive style – his attention focusing on the human figure, vehicles and machine parts, geometric forms and animals. The first thing that greets you when you enter is his enormous sculpture of *Vulcan*, towering over you like some monstrous android. Other works by him include a bronze entitled *Daedalus on Wheels* and a pen-and-ink *Fisherman and Wife*. Paolozzi also gave the gallery the contents of his London studio, which has now been recreated at the gallery. Amid a fascinating clutter of moulds, waxes, plasters and finished bronzes lies the simple, raised platform where he slept, and the atmosphere is such that it appears as though he has just stepped out for a quick walk.

The gallery is home to significant collections of **Dadaist** and Surrealist art. The Dada movement emerged during the First World War, and consisted of artists who wanted to attack the genteel cultural values that they felt were responsible for the war. **Max Ernst** described the movement as 'a rebellious upsurge of vital energy and rage'. The name

'Dada' was selected at random from a dictionary and chosen because it was a nonsense word. The work of several leading Dadaists, including Marcel Duchamp, Francis Picabia, Max Ernst and Man Ray, line the walls of the gallery.

Surrealism blossomed from the Dada movement. Artists interested in the unconscious scoured junk shops in search of strange objects that they could display alongside their works. The gallery has exhibited their works in a way that reflects this fascination. There are major paintings by René Magritte, Salvador Dalí, André Masson and Paul Delvaux. Picasso closely associated himself with the Surrealists and among his works on display is the collage *Tête*, once belonging to the founder and leader of Surrealism, André Breton.

Getting there: 73 Belford Road. Tel: (0131) 624 6200; recorded information (0131) 332 2266. Open: Mon–Sat 1000–1700; Sun 1400–1700. Open longer during the Festival. Admission free; charges for special exhibitions.

Scottish National Gallery of Modern Art

Belford Road. Tel: (0131) 624 6200. Open: Mon–Sat 1000–1700; Sun 1400–1700. Extended during the Festival. Free admission; charges for special exhibitions.

There is something very relaxing about a visit to this gallery. Perhaps it is because you are slightly removed from the hubbub of the city centre, or maybe it is the tranquillity of the leafy grounds in which it is set. Whatever the reason, it is the sort of place where you want to linger.

Devoted to post-19th-century art, the gallery first opened in 1960 at **Inverleith House** in the **Royal Botanic Garden**. Having outgrown its home, it moved in 1984 to its present site, a former school designed in 1825. The grounds are popular on sunny afternoons and are dotted with sculptures, including works by **Sir Henry Moore**, **Barbara Hepworth**, **Anthony Caro** and **William Turnbull**.

The collection contains thousands of items and works are shown on a rotational basis, although the most important treasures are generally always on display. The major strengths of the collection are its works by **Scottish artists**, especially the **Colourists** – Peploe, Fergusson, Hunter and Cadell – and contemporary artists such as **Alan Davie** and **Adrian Wiszniewski**.

The gallery has something to suit all tastes: don't miss **Fernand Leger**'s bright and energetic representation of construction workers, entitled *The Constructors: the team at rest*; **Lucien Freud**'s fleshy and muscular painting, *Two Men*; and **Otto Dix**'s rather eerie work, *Nude Girl on a Fur*.

Many works are compellingly detailed, such as **R B Kitaj**'s enigmatic and dreamlike *If Not, Not*, a complex painting strewn with figures and images, including the gatehouse to Auschwitz. You can also see **Natalya Goncharova**'s moving comment on **anti-Semitism** and compassion, *Rabbi and Cat*.

The gallery contains some gentle, familiar images. Keep a look-out for **Roy Lichtenstein**'s Pop Art piece, *In the Car*, and **Andy Warhol**'s *Portrait of Maurice*, a perky dachshund. One that always raises a smile is **Duane Hanson**'s splendidly cruel *Tourists*, portraying a middle-aged couple who stare into the distance with their mouths wide open.

St Mary's Episcopal Cathedral

Palmerston Place. Tel: (0131) 225 6293. Open: Mon–Fri 0730–1800; Sat and Sun 0730–1700; opens until 2100 in summer.

This enormous Gothic-style church, not far from the Modern Art Gallery, merits a few minutes of your time. Designed in the late 1870s, it is considered to be the finest church erected in Scotland since the Reformation. Its three distinctive spires appear magical when floodlit at night.

Stockbridge

Stockbridge is a part of town that most tourists have yet to discover, even though it is only minutes from the city centre. It was originally a village – its name comes from the bridge that crossed the Water of Leith, often used by livestock. It was largely developed as a residential area by Sir Henry Raeburn, the Scottish portrait painter.

The village atmosphere is still in evidence and many young professionals now live here. You could easily spend several hours browsing in the shops and there are plenty of cafés to relax in when you need to rest and refuel.

Ann Street

This Stockbridge street has been described as 'the most desirable address in Scotland' and was once likened to 'a Greek temple in a cottage garden'. It was built by Sir Henry Raeburn and named after his wife, Ann, a wealthy young widow whom he met when she came to his studio to have her portrait painted. The houses were originally sold for

between £200 and £1,200 (they now change hands for around half a million pounds) and soon became home to Edinburgh's eminent and eccentric society figures.

Number 29, the home of Professor John Wilson, a writer and moral philosopher, soon became a rendezvous for artists and the literati. His most colourful guest was Thomas de Quincey, the author of *Confessions of an Opium Eater*, who used to take around an ounce of opium a day. The street has other literary associations. One of the daughters of the family who lived at number 36 married Dr Joseph Bell, the surgeon who Sir Arthur Conan Doyle used as the model for his famous detective Sherlock Holmes. Ann Street is also said to have been the inspiration for J M Barrie's novel *Quality Street.*

St Stephen Street

This lovely little street is filled with individual and quirky shops. You can buy extravagant flowers, gorgeous designer homeware, art-nouveau jewellery, retro clothes and antiques. There is even a shop (which keeps eccentric opening hours) that sells all sorts of aged and antique lighting.

Fettes College

Just outside Stockbridge, in Inverleith, is the imposing structure of Fettes College, one of Scotland's most famous public schools *(no admission to the public).* It has been attended by many influential public figures, including the Prime Minister, Tony Blair, who is said to have hated it so much he tried to run away. Another old boy was Ian Fleming's fictional character James Bond.

> " If you're not a lawyer or an accountant you're thought of as bohemian. "
>
> **Giles Gordon, literary agent,**
> ***The Scotsman*, 1996**

Water of Leith

Water of Leith Centre, 24 Lanark Road. Tel: (0131) 455 7367 for information on the Water of Leith Walkway.

The Water of Leith is one of Edinburgh's hidden gems. From its source in the **Pentland Hills**, this river flows for over 35km, passing through Edinburgh and on to Leith, where it enters the **Firth of Forth**. Milling along the river dates back to the 12th century, and the water provided an important source of industrial power. The river had become polluted

and neglected, but in recent years, wildlife has returned and the walkway has been restored. Now you can walk along most of the river's length, from Balerno to Leith. Alternatively, you can simply stroll along a short section, perhaps joining the river by the Gallery of Modern Art and following the trail to Stockbridge.

The river is home to a diverse range of wildlife. You might spot herons, wagtails, dippers – and even the occasional kingfisher and otter.

Dean Village

Dean Village feels miles away from Edinburgh. It was an important milling village from the 12th century right up until the 19th century, and at one time 11 water mills were operated by the Baker's Guild, producing all the meal for Edinburgh. Picturesque and secluded, many of the old mills have now been converted into trendy flats.

Royal Botanic Garden

20A Inverleith Row. Tel: (0131) 552 7171. Open: daily 0930–dusk.

Founded in the 17th century, the Royal Botanic Garden has a reputation as one of the best-maintained gardens in the world. Grown in order to research the medicinal qualities of plants, it now covers 31 hectares (70 acres) of ground. The garden is lovely at all times of the year, but particularly in the spring when the rhododendrons are in bloom. Wander through the Chinese garden, the rock garden and some flamboyant glasshouses, filled with tropical palms, orchids and plants from arid lands.

At the centre of the gardens is Inverleith House, a Georgian mansion that hosts art exhibitions. The excellent café is very popular with locals at lunchtime.

St Bernard's Well

An unexpected sight on the river is this small Roman-style temple, complete with a statue of Hygeia, the Goddess of Health. Tradition has it that this mineral spring was discovered accidentally in 1760, by schoolboys fishing on the river. It quickly became popular as a 'cure' and was reputed to have the same healing qualities as the waters of Harrogate.

> " *Most disease of nature it quickly doth cure Except the disease that is got from a whore.* "
>
> **James Wilson, on the waters of St Bernard's Well, 1760**

Shopping

The West End and Stockbridge abound in interesting little shops and eateries hidden away in the most unlikely looking places.

Belinda Robertson Cashmere
22 Palmerston Place, West End. Tel: (0131) 225 1057. Showroom for designer cashmere garments where the public can buy knitwear at reduced prices.

Kate Wiggin
39 St Stephen Street, Stockbridge. Tel: (0131) 557 0560. Lovely one-off creations: furniture, ceramics, silk bags and lots more.

Montresor
35 St Stephen Street, Stockbridge. Tel: (0131) 220 6877. Gorgeous antique costume jewellery shop, specialising in art nouveau and art deco.

Napiers
35 Hamilton Place, Stockbridge. Tel: (0131) 343 6683. Napiers is a medical herbalist, established in 1860. The owners not only make the medicines available in the shop but also sell their own delicious smelling creams and cosmetics.

Eating and drinking

Bars and restaurants

Bar Roma
*39a Queensferry Street, West End.
Tel: (0131) 226 2977. £–££.* This
Italian restaurant is always busy,
lively and reliable.

La Cuisine d'Odile
*13 Randolph Crescent, West End. Tel:
(0131) 225 5685. £.* On the bottom
floor of the French Institute, this lovely
little restaurant (unfortunately only
open for lunch) tantalises you with
delicious, freshly made French food.

Howies
*4/6 Glanville Place, Stockbridge.
Tel: (0131) 225 5553. ££.* One of
Edinburgh's most popular restaurant
groups, Howies dishes up imaginative
Scottish food in sleek surroundings.
Filo parcels are filled with blue cheese
and ratatouille, and wild boar bangers
come with mash and onion gravy.

The Indian Cavalry Club
*3 Atholl Place, West End. Tel: (0131)
228 3282. ££.* This is a pretty smart
restaurant, offering a real taste of the
Raj. The food is excellent and authentic.

Indigo Yard
*7 Charlotte Lane, West End.
Tel: (0131) 220 5603. ££.* Very
sought-after by the West End
crowd, this stylish restaurant
serves chic and cosmopolitan food.

Maison Hector
*47–9 Deanhaugh Street, Stockbridge.
Tel: (0131) 332 5328. ££.* Trendy
Stockbridge bistro, with a quirky
interior. It's a lively place to come
for a meal or a cup of coffee.

McEwan's The Mugwump
*24a Stafford Street, West End.
Tel: (0131) 225 7889. ££.* The
chef at this unusual restaurant
concocts an extraordinary range
of dishes from medieval pot-roasts
to Mexican *enchiladas*.

Restaurant at the Bonham
*35 Drumsheugh Gardens, West
End. Tel: (0131) 623 9319. ££.*
Contemporary, undiscovered restaurant
concentrating on tasty Scottish fare.

San Marco
*10 St Mary's Place, Stockbridge. Tel:
(0131) 332 1569. £–££.* A favourite
haunt of Stockbridge residents, San
Marco effortlessly whips up pure
Italian food in a friendly atmosphere.

Cafés

Pâtisserie Florentin
*5 North West Circus Place, Stockbridge.
Tel: (0131) 220 0225. £.* Browse
through the paper while sipping
coffee and eating croissants and
calorie-laced pastries.

Other genial cafés are located at the
Scottish National Gallery of Modern
Art The Dean Gallery and the Royal
Botanic Garden

Literary Edinburgh

From Treasure Island *to* Trainspotting, *Edinburgh has provided inspiration for writers over hundreds of years, and is rich in literary associations. Some writers were born here, such as Kenneth Grahame (who wrote* The Wind in the Willows*) and Sir Arthur Conan Doyle, the creator of* Sherlock Holmes. *Others were visitors struck by the city's beauty, such as Daniel Defoe and Charlotte Brontë.*

Robert Burns came here to be launched into high society, while the First World War poets Siegfried Sassoon and Wilfred Owen met at Craiglockhart, a military hospital that stood just outside the city.

One of the city's most famous writers is Sir Walter Scott, who could often be seen writing late into the night at his home in Castle Street. The city's main station, Waverley, is named after one of his books, and there is a monument to him on Princes Street.

A heart mosaic in the pavement outside St Giles' Cathedral indicates the site of the old Tolbooth Prison, immortalised by Scott in the *Heart of Midlothian*.

Edinburgh's dark respectability famously inspired Robert Louis Stevenson to write *Dr Jekyll and Mr Hyde* (*see page 52*). The author of *Treasure Island*, which was inspired by the pond in the garden of his childhood home, lived in Edinburgh for much of his life. And even when he moved to Samoa, in the hope that the climate would aid his recovery from tuberculosis, the city continued to feature in his letters and other writings.

The city's outward decency also stimulated Edinburgh-born author Dame Muriel Spark into writing *The Prime of Miss Jean Brodie*. The genteel exterior of the central character, a prim schoolmistress, concealed an unhealthy regard for fascism.

Edinburgh's literary associations continue to flourish. Irvine Walsh's novel *Trainspotting* depicts the city's murky drug culture, and the city also features in the novels of Iain Banks, particularly in *Complicity*, which has now been made into a film. The children's publishing phenomenon, Harry Potter, was also created by an Edinburgh author. Joanne (J K) Rowling was an impoverished single mother when she wrote most of her first book, sitting in Nicolson's café in the city centre. The books have since made her one of Britain's richest women.

Edinburgh – Leith and Newhaven

For six hundred years Leith flourished as a port and the area retains a distinctive, maritime atmosphere, even though the old warehouses and docks are now crammed with lively bars and fashionable restaurants.

EDINBURGH – LEITH AND NEWHAVEN

Getting there: First Edinburgh **bus** *C3 runs along Leith Walk into Leith, then close to Newhaven Museum. A bus service to* Britannia *(No X50) leaves Waverley Bridge in central Edinburgh every 20 minutes.*

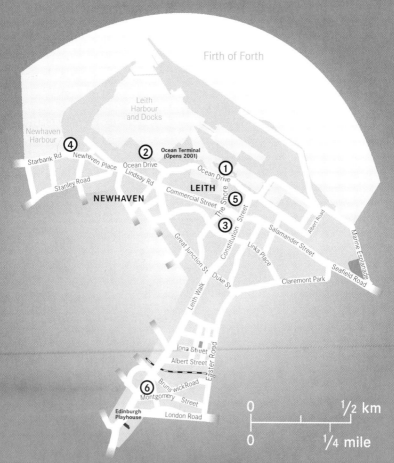

Firth of Forth

Leith Harbour and Docks

Newhaven Harbour

④ Starbank Rd

Newhaven Place

② Ocean Drive

Ocean Terminal
(Opens 2001)

Lindsay Rd

Stanley Road

NEWHAVEN

Ocean Drive

①

LEITH

Commercial Street

⑤

The Shore

③

Constitution Street

Links Place

Salamander Street

Albert Road

Marine Esplanade

Seafield Road

Claremont Park

Great Junction St

Duke St

Leith Walk

Iona Street

Albert Street

Easter Road

⑥ Montgomery Street

Brunswick Road

Edinburgh Playhouse

London Road

0 ————— ½ km

0 ————— ¼ mile

① *Bars and restaurants*

Leith has loads of funky places to eat, and more establishments are opening up all the time. There is something to suit every pocket, from traditional bars to fine fish restaurants. **Pages 80-1**

② Britannia

The former Royal Yacht *Britannia* is now berthed at Leith. Here's your chance to see the Queen's bedroom and the State Dining Room where the Royal Family entertained everyone from Rajiv Gandhi to President Clinton. **Pages 74–5**

③ *Lamb's House*

A wealthy merchant lived here in the 17th century. Today there are plans to run walking tours from the house and to open some of it as a museum, allowing Leith's history to come alive. **Page 78**

④ *Newhaven Heritage Museum*

A tiny but fascinating museum in the old fishing village of Newhaven gives you a revealing insight into the customs, superstitions and routines of the local fishermen and fishwives. **Page 78**

⑤ *The Shore*

This pretty street is right on the river in the heart of Leith. An atmospheric mix of flats, bars and restaurants, which springs to life on a fine day. **Page 79**

⑥ *Valvona and Crolla*

This award-winning Italian deli is an Edinburgh institution. Its inviting interior is crammed with everything from wine, balsamic vinegar and olive oil to delicious fresh pasta and cheese. **Page 77**

73

Britannia

You don't have to be a dedicated royal-watcher to enjoy a visit to Britannia *– she is a fascinating part of modern history and the last in a long line of Royal Yachts, stretching back to the reign of Charles II in the 17th century.*

Launched in 1953, she became the most famous ship in the world and was used by the Royal Family for state visits, holidays and honeymoons. By the 1990s she was showing her age, but a refit was ruled out as too expensive. She was decommissioned in December 1997 and opened to the public in October 1998 – a decision that did not please all members of the Royal Family: reportedly, Princess Anne wanted her scuttled.

Britannia appears smaller than you might expect, but she was a floating palace and a refuge for the Royals. The Queen once commented that the Royal Yacht was the one place in which she could relax. In contrast to every other Royal residence, the Queen and Prince Philip were involved with every detail of *Britannia*'s design – even down to the choice of door handles. A visit here gives you a unique peek at the private face of the family and the simplicity of their taste may surprise you.

Life on board *Britannia* seems to have been a strange mix of formality and frugality. The Drawing Room is comfortable, but not sumptuous, with ageing, chintzy sofas and a thick carpet. It is filled with fresh flowers, as it was whenever the Royal Family was on board. Bolted to the floor in one corner is a baby grand piano, once played by Sir Noel Coward.

The Dining Room was the location for state banquets where the Queen entertained guests such as Nelson Mandela, Sir Winston Churchill and Bill Clinton. The table, which is set for dinner and could seat 56 people, is not the original – Prince Philip had that removed when the yacht was decommissioned. It would take three hours to lay all the places for a state banquet and the position of every piece of cutlery was carefully measured with a ruler.

Most revealing of all are the Royal bedrooms. The Queen and the Duke of Edinburgh had separate rooms, furnished by narrow single beds and linked by a connecting door. The rooms have a functional appearance: there are no duvets; instead the beds are made up with sheets and blankets. The Queen's sheets turn out to be ancient (they were originally bought for Queen Victoria's bedroom), although they are all specially tailored and embossed with her personal monogram, 'H M The Queen'.

There is only one double bed on board, in a cabin used by honeymoon couples such as Prince Charles and the late Diana, Princess of Wales.

75

You also learn a little (some would argue not nearly enough) about life for the crew of *Britannia*, which appears to have been a disciplined routine of cleaning and polishing. The decks had to be meticulously scrubbed – in silence – before 0800 each morning, and if a crew member met one of the Royal Family, he had to stand stock-still and stare straight ahead until they had passed.

Getting there: 100 Ocean Drive, Leith. Tel: (0131) 555 5566; www.royalyachtbritannia.co.uk. Open: daily 1030–1630; some restrictions in winter. You are advised to pre-book your ticket by telephone 0900–1730 daily. ££.

Leith Walk

Until recently it was only the most adventurous visitor who came to Leith, as it was renowned for its rough character and seedy red-light district. Although just minutes from the city centre, this ancient port became part of Edinburgh as late as 1920 and therefore has its own distinctive heritage and character. Older people still resent being 'lumped together' with Edinburgh and refer to themselves as 'Leithers'.

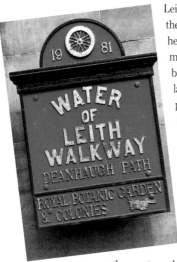

Leith enjoys a rich history as a wine port: the Romans stored wine for their legions here during the 1st century AD and in medieval times French religious orders based in Edinburgh used the dock to land wines imported from home. Trade prospered, especially since Leith also exported dried fish to France – in return, the ships would arrive back laden with local wine.

In the 18th and 19th centuries Leith enjoyed a worldwide reputation for its high standards of shipbuilding but when iron hulls replaced wooden ones, it was unable to compete with other ports and the industry gradually died. The town fell into decline and by the 1970s was a sad and derelict area, known more for its red-light district than for anything else.

In recent years Leith has undergone a renaissance, although it still retains its red-light district. The lovely old buildings are filled with trendy bars and restaurants and have been converted into smart flats for young professionals.

Drum Complex

Greenside Place, top of Leith Walk.

This site is set to become a £50-million film complex. When it is built it should contain restaurants, a fitness centre and a casino. Warners believe it will bring world premières to Edinburgh.

Sherlock Holmes Statue

Picardy Place, top of Leith Walk.

Many people pass by without noticing this statue of the famous detective, Sherlock Holmes, created by Sir Arthur Conan Doyle, who was born nearby at 11 Picardy Place (now demolished). Conan Doyle drew inspiration for the character of Sherlock Holmes from Dr Joseph Bell, an Edinburgh physician. The stories were so popular that when the author tired of his creation and tried to kill him off, he was compelled to revive him. Although remembered for Sherlock Holmes, Conan Doyle preferred his historical romances. He served as a doctor in the Boer War and was knighted for writing a pamphlet that corrected enemy propaganda.

Valvona and Crolla

19 Elm Row, Leith Walk. Tel: (0131) 556 6066. Open: Mon–Wed and Sat 0800–1800, Thur and Fri 0800–1930, closed Sun.

People have been known to step inside this Italian delicatessen and not emerge for hours. It is an independent family business, run by the descendants of the Crolla family who started the firm in 1934. The family's Edinburgh origins date back to the early 1860s when Benedetto Valvona, an Italian immigrant, opened a shop in the city. It's a great shop to come and browse, although it will be filled to bursting with locals on a Saturday. It has won many awards for its wines over the years – over 600 Italian varieties are on sale alone. Among other things, you can also find fresh pasta, vegetables, balsamic vinegar, olive oil, cheese and chocolate – the list is endless. There's even a café at the back of the shop where you can get a real cappuccino.

Lamb's House

Water Street, Leith.

This 17th-century merchant's house oozes with character.

Leith Links was a golf course as early as the 15th century. It established the rules of golf, years before they were formalised at St Andrews.

Although it has been used for many years as an old folks' day centre, there are plans afoot to open it up as a museum telling Leith's story. It may also be used as a base for walking tours of the area. Some say that Mary, Queen of Scots stayed here on her return from France in 1561. This seems unlikely as the house hadn't been built by this date.

Newhaven Heritage Museum

24 Pier Place, Newhaven Harbour. Tel: (0131) 551 4165. Open: Mon–Sun noon–1645. Admission free.

Newhaven lies a bit further along the coast from Leith and is well off the tourist trail. However, this little museum, next to Harry Ramsden's restaurant, gives a vivid insight into the lives of the local community. There are displays on Newhaven's origins as a naval dockyard, when it built ships such as *The Great Michael*, the largest vessel of its time. Lots of photographs and artefacts associated with the fishing industry adorn its rooms, and children will love being able to try on the traditional clothes. When you listen to the local people's taped accounts of their lives, it is hard to imagine that this close-knit fishing community is so near to Edinburgh.

Ocean Terminal

Tel: (0131) 555 8888.

This £100-million development next to *Britannia* is due to open in October 2001. It will welcome to Edinburgh cruise liners from around the world, and house a cinema, a conference centre, several hotels, specialist fashion shops and a Conran restaurant. It is just one part of the continued redevelopment of Leith that will also include the building of thousands of new waterfront houses, many of which have already been attracting the attention of such celebrities as Sean Connery

The Shore

The Shore is one of the most atmospheric parts of Leith. There are plenty of bars and restaurants to eat in, or you can just stroll lazily along beside the Water of Leith. There is a possibility that static vessels will be moored here as part of a larger Water Village development. The planners want to encourage more businesses to operate from boats and barges; erect a performance platform on which shows can be staged; and turn the Old Custom House into a Maritime Heritage Centre.

EDINBURGH – LEITH AND NEWHAVEN

Shopping

The opening of Ocean Terminal will introduce many smart new shops to Leith. At present you have to search a bit to find the interesting shops, but there are a few around.

Flux
55 Bernard Street, Leith. Tel: (0131) 554 4075. Lovely shop selling all sorts of arts and crafts. Look for the richly coloured wax lamps and interior panels, hand-thrown *raku* work and unusual metal flowers. A place to come to seek out up-and-coming artists.

First Choice Fabrics
7–8 Albert Place, Leith. Tel: (0131) 554 8754. This friendly shop on Leith Walk sells all sorts of gorgeous Asian suits, shawls and sari fabric.

Eating and drinking

Leith is one of Edinburgh's best areas for drinking and dining. It is noted for its fish restaurants, which are of an extremely high standard.

Bars and restaurants

Bar Sirius
Dock Place, Leith. Tel: (0131) 555 3344. £. Trendy-style bar, where you can come for a drink or a meal. The food is light and innovative, and may include dishes such as Thai seaweed with feta cheese, as well as classic British dishes.

Daniel's Bistro
88 Commercial Street, Leith. Tel: (0131) 553 5933. ££. There's a lively atmosphere in this French restaurant that lists some Alsatian specialities on the menu, as well as choices for vegetarians. You'll have to book at weekends.

Daruma-Ya
82 Commercial Street, Leith. Tel: (0131) 554 7660. ££. Sought-after Japanese restaurant where you can sample *sushi*, *tempura* and other authentic dishes.

Fishers
1 The Shore, Leith. Tel: (0131) 554 5666. ££. At the base of Leith's old signal tower, this fish restaurant is well patronised by those in the know – Tony Blair followed a trend, rather than set it, when he ate here on a visit to Edinburgh.

Fitzhenry

19 Shore Place, Leith. Tel: (0131) 555 6625. ££. This restaurant specialises in all those ingredients that you never dared – or wanted – to taste, such as pig's head or offal. If you aren't feeling that adventurous, it has also begun to offer more 'conventional' dishes.

Gulnar's Passage to India

46 Queen Charlotte Street, Leith. Tel: (0131) 554 7520. £–££. There's a strong Middle-Eastern atmosphere in this imaginative restaurant. The belly dancer on Saturday nights pulls in large crowds.

Harry Ramsden's

Newhaven Fish Market, Newhaven Harbour. Tel: (0131) 551 5566. £. Come here for delicious, old-fashioned fish, chips and mushy peas. Regular opera nights are held, when the Scottish Operatic and the Northern Operatic Societies take turns to entertain diners. They're great value but you'll need to book in advance.

King's Wark

36 The Shore, Leith. Tel: (0131) 554 9260. ££. The King's Wark dates back to the 17th century and has bags of character. It majors on fish and game dishes.

Malmaison Brasserie

1 Tower Place, Leith. Tel: (0131) 468 5000. ££. This brasserie is part of the Malmaison hotel, located in a restored seamen's hostel. Great French food is served in very sophisticated surroundings.

The Raj

The Shore, Leith. Tel: (0131) 553 3980. £–££. Large, airy Indian restaurant that is well established in Leith, with several house specialities worth investigating.

Ristorante Tinelli

139 Easter Road, Leith. Tel: (0131) 652 1932. ££. Located out of the centre of Leith, this Italian restaurant has a deserved reputation and produces high-quality food that Italians would wolf down.

The Rock

78 Commercial Street, Leith. Tel: (0131) 555 2225. ££. Steaks prove a winner at this popular converted warehouse space.

The Ship on the Shore

24–6 The Shore, Leith. Tel: (0131) 555 0409. ££. A comfortable restaurant, with a distinctly nautical feel, offers a wide choice of fish dishes, as well as vegetarian options.

The Shore Bar and Restaurant

3/4 The Shore, Leith. Tel: (0131) 553 5080. ££. A regular hang-out for the locals, it's constantly buzzing here. The menu always features fresh food that is in season and may include fish such as squid or sea bass.

Skippers

1a Dock Place, Leith. Tel: (0131) 554 1018. ££. Another great Leith fish restaurant, serving favourites such as fishcakes and Dover sole. Make sure you book before you go.

The Vintners Room

The Vaults, 87 Giles Street, Leith. Tel: (0131) 554 6767. ££. Loads of atmosphere in this old claret-auction house, which is candlelit at night. The food is French, centring on fish and game.

The Waterfront

1c Dock Place, Leith. Tel: (0131) 554 7427. ££. Relaxed bar and restaurant that dishes up meat and veggie dishes, as well as the ubiquitous fish dishes. Sit outside on a sunny day and soak up the views.

Scotland's Parliament

The first elections to a Scottish parliament for nearly 300 years took place on 6 May 1999. They followed an earlier referendum in which the majority of people voted for a devolved parliament.

Scotland's former parliament was dissolved when the English and Scottish parliaments became one through the **Act of Union** of 1707. The **crowns** of England and Scotland had already been united, in 1603, when the Scottish King, **James VI**, also became **James I of England**. For another century, however, the two countries remained very different, with England's parliament, for instance, enjoying far more powers than Scotland's, which was largely controlled by the King. In fact, James I once boasted in London: 'here I sit and govern Scotland with my pen; I write and it is done'.

Nor did the two countries always agree on their choice of monarch. Scotland, for example, crowned **Charles II** as its King several years before he was restored to the English throne in 1660. Matters came to a head when it looked as though **Queen Anne** would die without leaving a direct heir. The English wanted the throne to pass to a Hanoverian; the Scots disagreed. Concerned at the constitutional implications – and scared that war might break out – English ministers proposed the **political union** of the two countries.

EDINBURGH – LEITH AND NEWHAVEN

Years of famine, coupled with heavy financial losses suffered after a disastrous attempt to establish a trading company on the Isthmus of Darien in Panama, meant that many in the Scottish Parliament saw the benefits of such an arrangement. Needless to say, support for the loss of Scottish independence was not unanimous. Lord Belhaven declared: 'Good God. What, is this an entire surrender?' After unification, Scotland retained its own legal and educational systems and church.

During the 1990s, the campaign for Scottish self-government gathered momentum, as the Scots increasingly came to resent the distant parliament in Westminster. The unpopularity of the Thatcher government fuelled this antipathy – particularly when the hated poll tax (a tax that was not adjusted in line with income) was introduced to Scotland long before it was levied in England and Wales. Following the 1999 elections, the new Scottish Parliament has 129 MSPs (Members of the Scottish Parliament) and has the power to pass legislation and to alter the rate of tax. Scotland is still represented in the Westminster Parliament, however, which retains control of defence and foreign policy.

" When I consider this Affair of an Union betwixt the Two Nations … I find my Mind crowded with a variety of very Melancholy Thoughts. "

**Lord Belhaven
on the 1707
Act of Union**

Glasgow – city centre

Glasgow's city centre crackles with energy and its bold, warm buildings reflect the Victorian confidence in what was once 'the second city of the empire'.

85

Getting there: most **buses** pass through the city centre.
First Glasgow buses 20, 41 and 66 go to George Square
and past the Glasgow School of Art and the Tenement
House. Buses 5, 12, 18, 20, 40, 41, 56 and 57 pass close
to Princes Square. Nearest **underground** stops are
St Enoch for Princes Square and Cowcaddens for the
School of Art and the Tenement House.

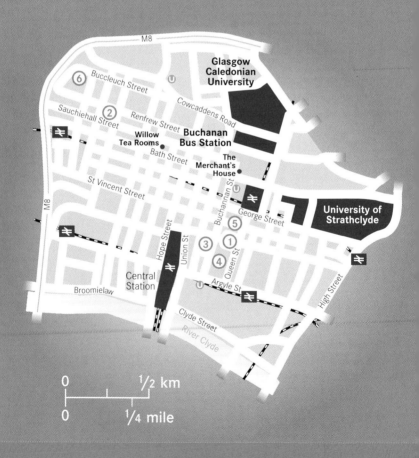

GLASGOW – CITY CENTRE

① The Gallery of Modern Art

Housed in the former Royal Exchange, this gallery contains a fresh, yet accessible, collection of contemporary paintings, photographic prints and sculptures. Artists exhibited range from Beryl Cook to Bosnian war artist Peter Howson. **Page 94**

② Glasgow School of Art

This sleek, angular building with its bold wrought-ironwork is widely acknowledged as the greatest achievement of the architect Charles Rennie Mackintosh. Still one of Britain's most prestigious art colleges, you can view the interior on a student-led tour. **Pages 90–1**

③ The Lighthouse

Scotland's Centre for Architecture, Design and the City, The Lighthouse is an imaginative conversion of the old *Glasgow Herald* building, designed by none other than Charles Rennie Mackintosh. Changing exhibitions show an innovative flair, while there is a permanent Mackintosh Interpretation Centre, dedicated to the work and legacy of the city's most famous architect. **Page 92**

④ Princes Square

This seriously stylish shopping centre boasts a Mackintosh-influenced interior and bears no resemblance to the faceless malls you can find on any high street. The shops sell designer clothes, accessories and crafts. **Page 93**

⑤ Shopping

Glaswegians love to shop, especially for clothes; consequently the city centre is the ideal place for a spot of retail therapy. The Buchanan Street area is a particularly good hunting-ground, but there are also specialist outlets such as Victorian Village in West Regent Street, where you can root out all sorts of antique jewellery and curios. **Page 96**

⑥ Tenement House

This immaculately preserved Glaswegian tenement provides a fascinating peep into the life of its owner, Miss Agnes Toward, who lived here for over forty years and never seemed to throw anything away. **Page 89**

87

Tourist information
11 George Square. Tel: (0141) 204 4400; e mail: enquiries@seeglasgow.com.
Glasgow's Tourist Information Centre is conveniently located in George Square at the heart of the city.

Around Sauchiehall Street

Sauchiehall Street is one of the most important shopping streets in the city and always bustles with Glaswegians searching for a bargain. It takes its name from 'sauchie haugh', meaning 'an area or a meadow of willows', although it is now impossible to imagine that this was ever a rural area.

Grecian buildings

Make sure you look up as you're walking along, otherwise you will miss the chance to admire some of the city's most interesting buildings, such as the Grecian Buildings. Now housing the Centre for Contemporary Arts, this was originally a commercial warehouse, designed with characteristic flourish by Alexander 'Greek' Thomson – Victorian Glasgow's greatest architect. His work, somewhat overshadowed by that of Mackintosh, was influenced by the classical architecture of ancient Greece, which he then reinterpreted with a practical and contemporary touch.

Willow Tea Rooms

217 Sauchiehall Street. Tel: (0141) 332 0521; www.willowtearooms.co.uk.

There's more distinctive architecture at the Willow Tea Rooms, an accurate reconstruction of Miss Cranston's famous tearooms, designed by Charles Rennie Mackintosh. It is easy to pass by, as the ground floor is occupied by a jeweller's, but once you stop and step back you can appreciate its clean, fresh appearance. Much of the original interior has survived, the unifying design theme being the willow tree, inspired by the meaning of the word 'Sauchiehall'. Mackintosh designed everything, from the tables and chairs to the teaspoons and menus.

McLellan Galleries

Tel: (0141) 332 7521.

Also on Sauchiehall Street are the McLellan Galleries, built as an art gallery in 1856, and now used for a variety of temporary displays. These may range from displays of local art to international, touring exhibitions.

The Tenement House

145 Buccleuch Street. Tel: (0141) 333 0183. Open: Mar–Oct, Mon–Sun 1400–1700. ££.

Just a few minutes' walk away is the Tenement House, virtually unchanged since its original owner, Miss Agnes Toward, left when she was taken into hospital in 1965. Tenement flats formed the bedrock of housing in Glasgow and varied in size from those having one room – often used to house a whole family – to seven-room apartments for the affluent middle classes. Miss Toward moved into the house with her mother in 1911 and it almost feels as though she has only just left. You can see everything, from the box-bed in the kitchen in which she slept, to an unopened pot of homemade jam, labelled 'Plum 1929'.

> " Glasgow is indeed a very fine city … In a word 'tis the cleanest and beautifullest and best built city in Britain, London excepted. "
>
> **Daniel Defoe (1660– 1731), *A Tour through the Whole Island of Great Britain***

Glasgow School of Art

Not only is this one of the oldest and most prestigious art schools in the country (past students include Robert Colquhoun, Ken Currie and actor Robbie Coltrane), it is also Charles Rennie Mackintosh's architectural masterpiece. The School dates back to 1845, and had expanded so much by 1896, that a new building was needed. The governors set up a competition to design it, which was won by Mackintosh, one of the School's ex-students, aged only 28 at the time.

From the outside it is striking in its simplicity, any severity enlivened by Mackintosh's distinctive wrought-ironwork. It is well worth taking one of the student-led tours, shepherding you inside and giving you the opportunity to see some of the most impressive rooms (curricular activities mean that not all areas are guaranteed to be open to the public).

Rooms you may see include the Director's Room, the earliest of Mackintosh's sleek, white rooms, and the deliciously light and airy Mackintosh Room, designed as a boardroom. There is also the Furniture Room, once a storeroom and now filled with slim Mackintosh chairs and bedroom furniture that once belonged to the architect and furniture from Miss Cranston's Tearooms. The most famous room is the two-storey Library with fitted bookcases, dark wooden desks and angular light fittings. With a building such as this to study in, it is little wonder that Glasgow is still producing inventive and innovative young artists.

Getting there: 167 Renfrew Street. Tel: (0141) 353 4526. Entry by guided tour only: Mon–Fri 1100 and 1400, Sat 1030 and 1130; extra tours in July and August. Pre-booking advisable. ££.

> " *Glasgow's citizens are larger than life. They live life as though it was a movie, and their wit is rapid-fire.* "

John Millar, journalist

The Lighthouse

11 Mitchell Lane. Tel: (0141) 221 6362; e mail: enquiries@thelighthouse.co.uk; www.thelighthouse.co.uk. Open: Mon, Wed, Fri, Sat 1030–1800; Tues 1100–1800; Thur 1030–2000; Sun 1200–1700. Admission free, except for the Mackintosh Interpretation Centre (£).

Food packaging, toilet-roll holders, computers, chairs, exhibitions on urban regeneration – you might come across any of these here. As Scotland's Centre for Architecture, Design and the City, The Lighthouse showcases the breadth of activities of the world of architecture and design, and although that may sound a bit 'worthy', it's certainly not dull. The centre is the legacy of Glasgow's year as UK City of Architecture and Design in 1999. The building, constructed in 1893–5 by Charles Rennie Mackintosh, for the *Glasgow Herald* newspaper, was his first public commission. When the paper moved premises, the building stood empty for years.

Now it's one of the hippest places in the city. Appropriately one gallery is permanently devoted to the Mackintosh Interpretation Centre, leading to the Mackintosh Tower, which has spectacular views across the city. The ground floor of the building is home to the trendy blue bar café.

Princes Square

48 Buchanan Street. Tel: (0141) 221 0324. Shops open: Mon–Sat 1000–1900;
Sun 1200–1700; restaurants open: Mon–Sat 1000–midnight; Sun 1200–1700.

More urban regeneration here, in the city's most distinctive
shopping centre, set in a once run-down 19th-century
courtyard. Lots of shiny wood and gleaming shop fronts
give the centre an up-market feel, and there are plenty
of restaurants and cafés if you need to rest your feet.
The central well is dominated by a replica of **Foucault's
Pendulum**, the device used to prove that the earth rotated
on its axis. Stores to explore include Whistles, Ted Baker,
Calvin Klein, Penhaligons and Karen Millen.

" *It is no cliché to say that Glasgow is a friendly city and Edinburgh a place
in which it is hard to make friends.* "

Jack McLean, *The Scotsman*, 1997

The Gallery of Modern Art

Queen Street. Tel: (0141) 229 1996. Open: Mon–Thur and Sat 1000–1700;
Fri and Sun 1100–1700. Admission free.

Once home to a rich tobacco merchant and later the Royal
Exchange, this rather grand building now houses the city's
largest collection of modern
works of art. Galleries are
themed on the elements of
Fire, Earth, Water and Air.
Artists whose work is exhibited
include Peter Howson, a
graduate of the Glasgow
School of Art, who became
the Imperial War Museum's
war artist in Bosnia. His
picture, *Patriots*, of three
aggressive, loutish men
and their dogs, portrays his
feelings about machismo
and patriotism. Exploring
a similar theme is Ken
Currie's *The Bathers*,
which explores xenophobia
and intolerance. You can
also see some photographs
by Mathias Kauage
from Papua New Guinea,
and Henri Cartier-
Bresson

The collection is fresh
and unintimidating and
is a great introduction to modern art for those
who know little about it. The museum is not afraid to exhibit
'popular' artists. Beryl Cook's cheery fat lady in *By the
Clyde* and Avril Paton's *Windows in the West*, a peek into
a Glasgow tenement, are also on show.

The Merchant's House

7 West George Street. Tel: (0141) 221 8272. Tours available if there are no functions on; either call first and check that it is open or take a chance. Go to the Collector's office on the ground floor. Open: Mon–Fri 0900–1700; closed for lunch 1300–1400. Admission free.

This grand Glaswegian institution is the old Merchants' Guild, representing the mercantile community. Today it is principally concerned with charitable duties and lets its rooms out for meetings and functions. The interior is well worth a look with dark wooden panelling and richly coloured stained-glass windows.

Shopping

Borders
98 Buchanan Street. Tel: (0141) 222 7700. Book lovers will never want to leave this excellent bookshop – it's even got a great café so you can stop for sustenance while browsing through the very good selection of Scottish titles.

Buchanan Galleries
Buchanan Street. Tel: (0141) 333 9898. This enormous shopping centre contains all the usual suspects: a huge branch of John Lewis and some more unusual stores such as Mango, which sells Spanish designer clothes.

Men can get kitted out at stores such as **Diesel** (*116–20 Buchanan Street; tel: (0141) 221 5225*) and **Aspecto** (*34 Gordon Street; tel: (0141) 248 6900*). Then there's **Slaters** (*165 Howard Street; tel: (0141) 552 7171*), the world's largest menswear store – every man in Glasgow must have come here at some time.

Princes Square Sleek and glossy shopping centre (*see page 93*).

Saratoga Trunk
3rd Floor, 61 Hydepark Street. Tel: (0141) 221 4433. Open: weekdays only. Get a taxi as it's a bit of a walk from the centre. You'll need to ring the day before to come to this enormous old warehouse, as they are sometimes busy finding clothes for film crews. It's stuffed with clothing, linens, jewellery and hatboxes, from Victorian times to the present day, and it's a wonderful place to root out bargains. They supplied Madonna's jewellery for the film *Evita*.

Victorian Village Antiques
93 West Regent Street. Tel: (0141) 332 0808. Come here for gorgeous antique and costume jewellery, delicate retro clothes and dainty evening bags.

Eating and drinking

The city centre is full of bars and restaurants and there is something to suit everyone – from cool and trendy to chic and sophisticated. They can get busy, especially at weekends, so it is advisable to book ahead.

Bars and restaurants

78 St Vincent Street
78 St Vincent Street. Tel: (0141) 248 7878. ££. Contemporary Scottish food with traditional dishes such as *cullen skink* (a soup) and roasted meats, all given a modern twist.

Bar 10
10 Mitchell Lane. Tel: (0141) 572 1446/1448. £–££. There is an emphasis on vegetarian food at this style bar, which serves breakfast as well as unusual sandwiches and snacks. On Sundays there is live music – generally folk or jazz.

blue bar café
The Lighthouse, Mitchell Lane. Tel: (0141) 204 2404. ££. Hip and trendy café producing soups and sandwiches, as well as more substantial meals.

Budda
142a St Vincent Street. Tel: (0141) 243 2212. ££. Relaxed atmosphere and good Scottish food. Come here for dishes such as roasted langoustines.

Casa
421–30 Sauchiehall Street. Tel: (0141) 332 4760. £–££. Stop off for coffee, sandwiches or light meals.

Popular and well-established **Chinese restaurants** are the **Amber Regent** (*50 West Regent Street; tel: (0141) 331 1655; ££*) and the **Ho Wong** (*82 York Street; tel: (0141) 221 3550; ££–£££*).

Corinthian
191 Ingram Street. Tel: (0141) 552 1101. ££. Bar and bistro in an enormous building that was once a bank.

The Drum and Monkey
93–5 St Vincent Street. Tel: (0141) 221 6636. ££. Another converted bank is now home to a bistro and bar, popular with business people.

Eurasia
150 St Vincent Street. Tel: (0141) 204 1150. ££–£££. Private parking available. One of Glasgow's newest style restaurants fuses Scottish produce with oriental herbs and spices. Sample dishes such as twice-baked sweetcorn soufflé with braised Asian greens and oyster sauce.

Fratelli Sarti

121 Bath Street and 133 Wellington Street. Tel: (0141) 204 0440. £–££. Sarti's is a real Glaswegian institution and a little piece of Italy. Try a creamy cappuccino or excellent Italian dishes, then soak up the atmosphere.

Malmaison

278 West George Street. Tel: (0141) 572 1001. ££. Established and popular brasserie offering a good-value, fixed-price menu, as well as à la carte.

Mojo

158a Bath Street. Tel: (0141) 331 2257. ££. Crowds of the young and chic descend here for Japanese food and unusual fish dishes.

Rogano

11 Exchange Place. Tel: (0141) 248 4055. £££. Rogano is seriously selective – you have to ring the bell for attention. It's famed as much for its décor as its food: the interior replicates the *Queen Mary* cruise ship. The café is slightly easier on the pocket.

Tun Ton

157 Hope Street. Tel: (0141) 572 1230. £–££. Tun Ton serves innovative fusion food, mixing flavours from all over the world but with an Asian slant. Drop in for a light lunch or dinner.

Yes

22 West Nile Street. Tel: (0141) 221 8044. ££. Cool, clean décor and Mediterranean-style food. Chic but relaxed.

Fast food

Ichiban Japanese Noodle Café

50 Queen Street. Tel: (0141) 204 4200. £. You won't go hungry at this place after an enormous bowl of noodles in delicious, clear soup.

99

GLASGOW – CITY CENTRE

Glasgow's architecture

Visit Glasgow for the first time, filled with preconceptions about city slums, and you are sure to be pleasantly surprised. Because it is essentially an industrial city, Glaswegians do not feel burdened by history and have always had a 'go for it' attitude to architecture. Although for a time the city became blackened with the smoke and grime of industry, it has now been cleaned up, and you can appreciate its distinctive mix of elegant grey, soft yellow and warm red buildings.

Little remains of medieval Glasgow, essentially an ecclesiastical city, but it is appropriately represented by the ancient **Cathedral**, which dates back to the 13th century (*see page 124*).

The next wave of construction took place during the mid-18th century, when traders in Glasgow began to benefit from the union with England (*see pages 82–3*). The **Merchant City** (*see pages 126–7*) was created, where tobacco, rum and sugar merchants erected their mansions and warehouses.

The buildings are confident and pragmatic, and seem to hold an aura of respectability, most notably, perhaps, in Robert Adam's refined Trades Hall (*see page 127*).

But Glasgow is, above all, a Victorian city, and its bold and confident Victorian architecture gives the city its distinctive appearance. Industrialisation meant that workers flooded into the city and were housed in tenement flats. Commercial life flourished: magnificent banks, insurance offices and shops were commissioned, along with flamboyant public buildings such as Kelvingrove Art Gallery and Museum (*see pages 110–11*). Many of the most interesting buildings of this time were designed by Alexander 'Greek' Thomson, who got his name from his interest in the architecture of Classical Greece, which he incorporated into his own work. One of his outstanding buildings is St Vincent Street Church.

101

Glasgow's most famous, and original, buildings were designed around the turn of the 20th century by Charles Rennie Mackintosh. His imaginative designs were revolutionary and instantly recognisable. Exteriors had clean, simple lines and elaborate ironwork; interiors were sleek, light and uncluttered. His masterpiece is the Glasgow School of Art (*see pages 90–1*).

" To the Glaswegian, art, like beauty, is in the eye of the beholder. "

Jimmy Reid, trade union activist, journalist and broadcaster

Nowadays the face of Glasgow is still changing. There are innovative homes and a new Science Centre in the pipeline, and with The Lighthouse as a Centre of Architecture, it looks as though Glaswegian architecture is set to continue to flourish.

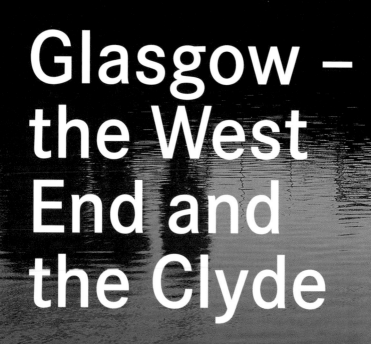

Glasgow – the West End and the Clyde

Funky and fashionable, the West End is dominated by the city's ancient university. Here you'll find some of Glasgow's finest museums and exuberant, warm, red sandstone buildings.

GLASGOW – THE WEST END AND THE CLYDE

Glasgow – the West End and the Clyde

*Getting there: the nearest **underground** stations are Kelvinhall and Hillhead. For the Tall Ship at Glasgow Harbour take the underground to Partick and walk – otherwise take a short taxi ride from the centre of town. **Buses** 9, 18, 20, 41, 62 and 66 run out here to the Byres Road, Kelvingrove Museums and the Botanic Gardens. Buses 44, 44A and 44D run by the Hunterian Museum.*

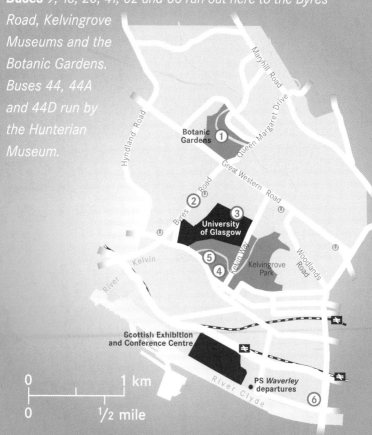

① Botanic Gardens

This cool, green oasis in the West End stretches invitingly along the River Kelvin. And you don't have to wait for good weather to visit: you can shelter from the rain in the world-famous glasshouses, which contain large collections of orchids, ferns and begonias. **Page 112**

② Byres Road

This is the student hub of the West End and its cosmopolitan air has led some to call it Glasgow's 'Latin Quarter'. Read the papers over a skinny *latte*, people-watch, then browse for bargains in the shops. **Page 108**

③ Hunterian Art Gallery and Museum

Scotland's oldest public museum is part of the university. As well as displays of fossils, coins and minerals, you can see Europe's largest collection of paintings by **Whistler**. **Pages 108–9**

④ Kelvingrove Art Gallery and Museum

You could lose yourself in this sprawling and elaborate Victorian building. Its huge upper galleries house one of the finest civic art collections in Britain, while the lower galleries exhibit everything from armour to natural history. **Pages 110–11**

⑤ Museum of Transport

Trains and boats and planes. Well, trains and ships anyway, in a museum that tells the story of transport on land and sea. Little boys – of all ages – find it irresistible. **Pages 112–13**

⑥ The Tall Ship at Glasgow Harbour

Imagine the salt spray in your face and the wind in your hair, when you go on board the *Glenlee*. One of only five Clyde-built sailing ships still afloat, it has been lovingly restored to its former glory. **Page 107**

105

Along the Clyde

'The Clyde made Glasgow – but Glasgow made the Clyde' goes the saying, revealing the close relationship between this city and its river.

Although the city grew from an important crossing point on the Clyde, the river was for centuries extremely shallow and therefore unnavigable. It was only with industrialisation at the end of the 18th century that engineers managed to deepen the river, allowing ships to sail from the Firth of Clyde to the city. The river quickly altered beyond all recognition, and docks and shipyards sprang up along its banks. Soon it was one of the most important industrial rivers in the world.

Over 35,000 ships have been launched from Clyde shipyards.

Shipbuilding was the most important industry on the river. Perhaps the most famous ships built here were the liners, the *Queen Mary*, the *Queen Elizabeth*, the *QEII* and the former Royal Yacht *Britannia*.

As the shipbuilding industry declined the shipyards along the Clyde began to close, and in recent years the river has looked rather mournful and neglected. However, there are plans for a massive redevelopment of a huge stretch of the river, extending from the Scottish Exhibition and Conference

Centre to the Clyde Tunnel. Called Glasgow Harbour, the plan is to demolish former dockside sheds and open up the river to leisure and commerce, with the establishment of shops, hotels, commercial businesses and houses. It looks as though the Clyde is about to rise again from the rusting remnants of the shipyards.

The Tall Ship at Glasgow Harbour

100 Stobcross Road. Tel: (0141) 339 0631; www.glenlee.co.uk.
Open: daily 1100–1700. ££.

The three-masted *Glenlee* is a Clyde-built sailing ship that has been carefully restored and is now a visitor attraction. *Glenlee* was launched in 1896 and circumnavigated the globe four times, sailing round Cape Horn fifteen times. She was saved from the scrapyard in 1992 by the Clyde Maritime Trust and is one of only five Clyde-built sailing ships in the world still afloat.

Not far from the *Glenlee* is the Scottish Exhibition and Conference Centre (SECC), where concerts and exhibitions of all types are held. Its latest addition is Sir Norman Foster's Clyde Auditorium, known locally as the 'Armadillo' due to its distinctive shape.

Waverley Paddle Steamer

Anderston Quay. Tel: (0141) 243 2224. ££.

Moored close to the city centre, the *Waverley* is the last sea-going paddle steamer in the world. She was launched in 1947 as a replacement for her namesake, which was sunk while rescuing troops from Dunkirk. As one of a number of Clyde pleasure boats, *Waverley* used to take holidaymakers and day-trippers on excursions 'doon the watter' to destinations such as Dunoon and Rothesay. Eventually the fleet declined but *Waverley* was saved from the breaker's yard and acquired by a charity for £1. She underwent a £3-million rebuild in 2000, reinstating her original 1947 appearance, and once again runs pleasure cruises during the summer. *(See excursions.)*

Byres Road

The Byres Road is the hub of the West End and is always thronged with students from the nearby university. Come here to explore the local shops or try some of the excellent bars and restaurants nearby. It's here that you'll find Curlers, a student haunt and reputedly the oldest pub in Glasgow. Some of the pub's famous drinkers included the Scottish poet and founder member of the Scottish National Party, Hugh MacDiarmid.

Hunterian Museum

University Avenue. Tel: (0141) 330 4221; www.gla.ac.uk/Museum.
Open: Mon–Sat 0930–1700; closed for public holidays. Admission free.

The oldest museum in Glasgow was established due to one man's passion for collecting. William Hunter, a wealthy

physician and ex-student of the university, gathered an enormous range of items during his lifetime, in particular medical specimens, books, coins and paintings. He bequeathed these to the university, as well as a sum of money with which to build a museum.

Naturally there is a strong educational bias to the museum but it still has much to interest the layman. The Geological Collection includes the so-called Bearsden Shark, a locally discovered fossil believed to be around 325 million years old. There is also a clutch of unhatched dinosaur eggs from China. In the Ethnographic Collection you can trace the development of the human race from the very earliest hominids, and there is also material gathered by Captain Cook on his voyages of the Pacific. The Coin Collection tells the story of the development of coinage.

Hunterian Art Gallery

University of Glasgow, 82 Hillhead Street. Tel: (0141) 330 5431; www.gla.ac.uk/Museum. Open: Mon–Sat 0930–1700; Mackintosh House closes daily 1230–1330. Admission free.

Light and airy, and not too big to be overwhelming, the Art Gallery houses the university's renowned art collection that grew from William Hunter's original bequest. Paintings from the 18th and early 19th centuries comprise works by Allan Ramsay, Sir Joshua Reynolds, George Stubbs and Gavin Hamilton's painting of the abdication of Mary, Queen of Scots. The French and Scottish collections include work by French artists Pissarro, Rodin and Boudin, and the Scottish landscape painter William McTaggart.

One of the gems of the gallery is its collection of paintings by the American, James McNeill Whistler – a collection that is rivalled only by that in the Freer Gallery, Washington. Many of his distinctive full-length portraits are displayed, as well as his famous murky pictures of the Thames. You can also see his palettes and specially made long-handled paintbrushes.

The university owns the world's largest collection of the work of Charles Rennie Mackintosh, Scotland's most famous architect, and the most unusual aspect of the gallery is the Mackintosh House, a faithful reconstruction of his Glasgow home.

The interiors contain the original fixtures and furniture and it is fascinating to see the extent to which Mackintosh paid attention to detail – even down to the umbrella stand and table runner. The most stunning room is the studio-drawing room, with its crisp white walls, furniture and thick white carpet.

" *Glasgow is undeniably a friendly city; her people are garrulous and talkative and welcoming and desperate, like all people who have been the object of much scorn, to show off a bit.* "

Jack McLean,
***The Scotsman*, 1997**

Kelvingrove Art Gallery and Museum

Scotland's most popular free attraction, this rich red sandstone building was the centrepiece of the 1901 Glasgow International Exhibition and has been a favourite with locals ever since.

Pending approval of its application for a National Lottery grant, the museum may be redesigned in order to rotate its collection of over one million artefacts and to incorporate more interactive exhibitions. If so, it will be closed for at least ten months, so check it's open before you visit.

The wonderful thing about Kelvingrove is the sheer range of its exhibits. You can find anything here, from dinosaurs and Victorian stuffed animals to a waterproof Inuit suit made from seal intestines. The museum also holds special exhibitions – the Dead Sea Scrolls were once displayed here.

Some of the collections in the museum are of particular note, not only for their content, but also for their historical value: some specimens were collected by David Livingstone,

the explorer and missionary who was also a naturalist. **Ethnographic exhibits** span all corners of the globe and contain masks from Africa, carved Maori figures and samurai clothing. **European displays** cover arms and armour, clocks, snuff-boxes and a fine collection of pewter.

The upper floor is devoted to the art collections, which include glass, ceramics and pottery. One gallery is devoted to the **Glasgow Style**, an innovative, decorative arts style that flourished during the 1890s and into the 20th century. **Charles Rennie Mackintosh** was at the heart of the movement and some of the furniture he designed for Miss Cranston's tearooms is on view, together with works by his wife, Margaret Macdonald, and other imaginative artists.

There is also a superb collection of paintings, drawings and sculpture – over 3,000 paintings alone. Most schools are represented, especially 17th-century Dutch and 19th-century French pieces, plus paintings by Scottish artists; there are so many fascinating pictures that it is hard to know where to look first. There is **Sandro Botticelli**'s painting of *The Annunciation*, **Van Gogh**'s *Portrait of Alexander Reid* and **Pieter Jansz Saenredam**'s austere and evocative portrayal of the *Interior of the Church of St Bavo, Haarlem*.

Don't miss paintings by **Seurat**, **Cézanne** and **Monet**, atmospheric landscapes by Scottish painters such as **William McTaggart**, and works by the **Scottish Colourists**. Pictures by the 'Glasgow Boys' give an insight into the city's lively, anti-establishment character, which often emerges in its art. This loosely knit group of artists came together in the late 1880s and rejected the conservatism and sentiment that ran through Scottish art at the time. Instead they painted earthy, realistic scenes of life and landscape, such as **James Guthrie**'s *Old Willie – the village worthy* and **William Kennedy**'s *The Deserter*.

Getting there: Kelvingrove, Argyle Street. Tel: (0141) 287 2699. Open: Mon–Thur and Sat 1000–1700; Fri and Sun 1100–1700. Admission free.

Botanic Gardens

730 Great Western Road. Tel: (0141) 334 2422. Gardens open: 0700–dusk; Kibble Palace open: summer 1000–1645; winter 1000–1615. Admission free.

In Victorian times, the fashionable and well connected would come to stroll in these extensive gardens, formed to provide a source of plant material for medical and botanical students at the university. Most of the world-famous glasshouses have been rebuilt in recent years and they contain fine displays of orchids, succulents, ferns and tropical plants. It's a great place to escape from the bustle of the busy West End streets, especially on a sunny day.

> " Glasgow is the pride of Scotland, and indeed it might very well pass for an elegant and flourishing city in any part of Christendom. "
>
> **Tobias Smollett (1721–71), Humphry Clinker**

There is a herb garden full of medicinal plants, an arboretum and a **Chronological Border**, where the plants are laid out according to the period in which they were introduced into Britain. The centrepiece of the Botanic Gardens is the **Kibble Palace**, an enormous Grade A listed glasshouse which was erected here in 1873. It was originally used for promenade concerts and public meetings – in fact, two British Prime Ministers, **William Gladstone** and **Benjamin Disraeli**, gave their rectorial addresses here when they became Rectors of the University of Glasgow. One wing of the Palace now contains a coffee shop and a visitor centre that often features art exhibitions. The Palace is due for major renovation work, which could be underway at the time you visit.

Museum of Transport

Kelvin Hall, 1 Bunhouse Road. Tel: (0141) 287 2720. Open: Mon–Thur and Sat 1000–1700; Fri and Sun 1100–1700. Admission free.

This is not just a museum of old cars and bikes but a peep into Glasgow's past. On the left, as you go in, is **Kelvin Street** – the recreation of an atmospheric Glaswegian street around 1938. Shop fronts lining the street include a pharmacy – complete with old medicine bottles and potions – a post office and a working Regal cinema.

Elsewhere in the museum, you will find some of the gleaming old **trams** that used to trundle around the city streets, old fire engines and – to trainspotters' delight – some railway locomotives. Interactive displays look at contemporary transport matters such as car crime. Then there are the commercial vehicles, including a milk float and steamroller and funny **old delivery vans** – presumably once driven by the motorist's favourite *bête noire*, the 'white van man'.

The fine **car collection** includes many Scottish-built models, as well as a Rolls Royce Phantom II, once owned by **Sir William Burrell** (whose legacy is the Burrell Collection). Many of the cars are displayed in a 'showroom' and you view them much the same as a potential purchaser would have done. Other models on show include a **Messerschmitt bubble car** and a Stanley Steamcar.

The **Clyde Room** is devoted to the river that made Glasgow the centre of the shipbuilding industry in the 19th century. Displays explain the history of shipbuilding on the Clyde and there is a huge collection of intricate model ships, many of them replicas of famous Clyde-built vessels. The *Cutty Sark* is here, along with the *Queen Mary* and the two *Queen Elizabeths*.

Eating and drinking

Funky style bars, fancy restaurants and friendly bistros jostle for your attention in the West End. Booking is advised as they can get very busy.

Bars and restaurants

Air Organic
36 Kelvingrove Street. Tel: (0141) 564 5200. ££. This trendy bar is a favourite with the beautiful people. Forget the 'knit your own vegetables' idea of organic food, the food is light and full of flavour with an Asian influence.

Axiom
154 Hydepark Street, Lancefield Quay. Tel: (0141) 221 2822. ££. Contemporary Scottish food served in stylish surroundings.

Brel
39–43 Ashton Lane. Tel: (0141) 342 4966. ££. Come to this fashionable, continental-type bar-restaurant for delicious Belgian food and, of course, a wide range of Belgian beers.

The Cabin
996–8 Dumbarton Road, Whiteinch. Tel: (0141) 569 1036. £££. People say that it feels like eating in someone's front room; large groups particularly love coming here. There's a real party atmosphere, with good fish dishes and game. But the evening's not complete until Wilma the waitress gets up to sing.

Cul-de-Sac
44–6 Ashton Lane, Hillhead. Tel: (0141) 334 4749. ££. Well-established restaurant offering crêpes, quality burgers and vegetarian options to the arty and cosmopolitan crowd of the West End.

Nairn's
13 Woodside Crescent. Tel: (0141) 353 0707. £££. This is celebrity chef Nick Nairn's restaurant, offering modern and chic Scottish cuisine.

Oblomov
372–4 Great Western Road. Tel: (0141) 339 9177. ££. Contemporary bar-restaurant with an eastern European theme. Oblomov was the first bar in Glasgow to serve absinthe.

One Devonshire Gardens
Devonshire Gardens. Tel: (0141) 339 2001. £££. This restaurant is located in Glasgow's most stylish hotel, much frequented by visiting celebrities. Its high-quality food has earned it a Michelin star – though the surroundings are so sumptuous that you could be forgiven for not noticing the food.

Puppet Theatre
11 Ruthven Lane. Tel: (0141) 339 8444. ££. Modern, Scottish food in romantic surroundings.

Stravaigin
28–30 Gibson Street. Tel: (0141) 334 2665. ££. Award-winning Scottish restaurant conjuring up delicious dishes made from the freshest produce. There is always one vegetarian and one fish choice.

Two Fat Ladies
88 Dumbarton Road. Tel: (0141) 339 1944. ££. Despite its rather unpromising name, this high-standard fish restaurant has a recipe for everything, from red snapper to oysters.

The Ubiquitous Chip
12 Ashton Lane, Hillhead. Tel: (0141) 334 5007. ££–£££. This was Glasgow's ground-breaking Scottish restaurant and it is still as popular as when it first opened. It has won many awards over the years and is noted for its game.

Other popular restaurants are Janssens (*1355 Argyle Street; tel: (0141) 334 9682; £–££*), which serves Dutch-style food, and The Living Room (*5–9 Byres Road; tel: (0141) 339 8511; £*).

The West End also has some excellent Indian restaurants. Try Ashoka West End (*1284 Argyle Street; tel: (0141) 339 3371; ££*), Killermont Polo Club (*2022 Maryhill Road; tel: (0141) 946 5412; ££*), Mother India (*28 Westminster Terrace, Sauchiehall Street; tel: (0141) 221 1663; ££*) or Shish Mahal (*66–8 Park Road; tel: (0141) 339 8256; ££*).

Coffee stop

Tinderbox
189 Byres Road. Tel: (0141) 339 3108. £. Sleek, metallic café serving great *lattes*, as well as sandwiches and snacks.

Shopping

Quirky shops abound here; look out for bargains.

Moon (*10 Ruthven Lane*) sells new labels in women's fashion, while Starry, Starry Night (*19 Downside Road*) stocks all sorts of second-hand delights. Then there is Retro in Otago Street for antiques and bric-a-brac and De Courcey's Arcade in Cresswell Lane, where you can rummage to your heart's content.

Glasgow Style

Glasgow Style may be hard to define but its presence can be felt in every aspect of city life. The term is strictly used to refer to the idiosyncratic type of art-nouveau design that appeared in the city in the late 19th and early 20th centuries. Initially influenced by contemporary designers such as William Morris and artists such as Aubrey Beardsley and Whistler, elements of Japanese art crept in, with simple forms and elongated lines. Designers began to use motifs taken from nature, such as roses and foliage. Eventually the distinctive designs appeared in pubs and shops, on stained glass and even on tiles.

The most significant exponent of this style was **Charles Rennie Mackintosh**, whose revolutionary buildings and interiors frequently attracted heavy criticism. His influence can still be felt throughout the city today, not only in buildings such as the Princes Square shopping centre, but also in a million pieces of jewellery, mugs and even bookmarks.

But the term 'Glasgow Style' can also be used much more loosely to try and encapsulate the city's distinctive lack of pretension, coupled with its energy, vitality and flair. The city's industrial past, the years of poverty and the cohesiveness of tenement housing (which was used by the wealthy middle classes as well as the poor) all combined to give the citizens a feeling of unity – as well as a need to make their voices heard. There is a sense of this style in the revitalisation of the buildings in the Merchant City and in the paintings of the so-called **'New Glasgow Boys'** – Adrian Wiszniewski, Peter Howson, Ken Currie and Steven Campbell – whose imaginative works burst on to the scene in the 1980s. You can hear the Glasgow Style in the sharp observations and quick-witted remarks made by people on the streets; you can feel the essence of it when you visit the stylish cafés, bars and bistros; and you can see proof of it by the way the people dress and their love for clothes and fashion. You don't have to scratch a Glaswegian very deep to find a committed shopaholic underneath: Glasgow Style is all about Glaswegian people.

117

" *I have heard a voice from across a crowded bar seeking information. 'Hey Jimmy, who was that b… who wrote Handel's Largo?* "

Jimmy Reid, trade union activist, journalist and broadcaster

Glasgow – the East End and Merchant City

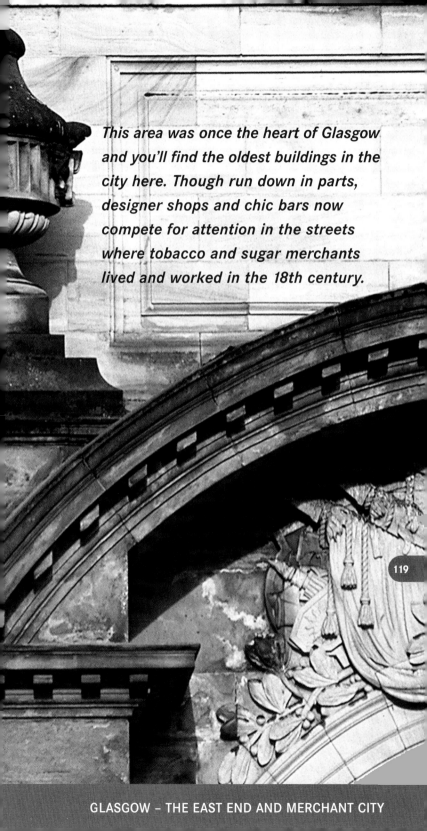

This area was once the heart of Glasgow and you'll find the oldest buildings in the city here. Though run down in parts, designer shops and chic bars now compete for attention in the streets where tobacco and sugar merchants lived and worked in the 18th century.

119

BEST OF
Glasgow – the East End and Merchant City

*Getting there: the Cathedral, Provand's Lordship and St Mungo's Museum are about a 10-minute **walk** from Queen Street Station and George Square. **Buses** 11, 12, 16, 38, 42, 51, 58 and 59 all run here. The Merchant City is adjacent to George Square. For the People's Palace and Templeton's Carpet Factory take bus 18 or 64 down London Road.*

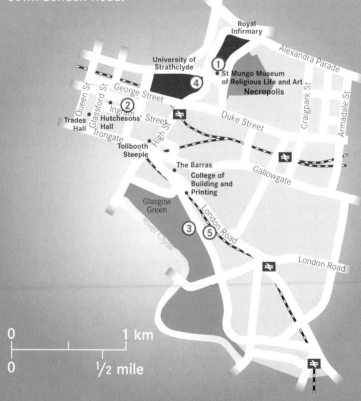

GLASGOW – THE EAST END AND MERCHANT CITY

① *Glasgow Cathedral*

This medieval church is something of a rarity – it is one of the few Scottish cathedrals to have survived the attentions of Protestant Reformers in the 16th century. **Page 124**

② *Italian Centre*

This is a seriously stylish shopping centre. Make sure you've got your credit card handy before you step over the threshold of the Italian designer stores. Alternatively, sip a cappuccino and watch the world go by.
Page 127

③ *People's Palace*

Here's a lusty peek into the history of Glasgow and its people. There are displays on everything from the 'steamie' (public laundry) to tenement living. There's even an introduction to local dialect, 'the patter'. **Pages 122–3**

④ *Provand's Lordship*

If this building could talk, it would doubtless tell a tale or two. Filled with period furnishing, it's the oldest house in Glasgow and dates back to 1471.
Page 125

⑤ *Templeton's Carpet Factory*

Although you can only view the exterior, this extraordinary and richly coloured building is well worth seeing. A former carpet factory, now a business centre, it was modelled on the **Doge's Palace** in Venice. **Page 123**

121

Glasgow Green

Glasgow's oldest park, Glasgow Green, has been common land since the 12th century. It was mainly used for grazing cattle and sheep until it became a public park in Victorian times. Much of East End life was played out here: political demonstrations, football and athletics, even the bleaching and washing of clothes.

In 1999, during Glasgow's year as City of Architecture and Design, the Green was chosen as the location for **Homes for the Future**. These are innovative new homes designed

by architects from around the world. They incorporate new technologies to create energy-efficient houses for the 21st century.

The Barras

The Barras Centre, London Road. Open: Sat and Sun 0900–1700.

You'll have plenty of chance to hear 'the patter' at this famous outdoor market. It's the place to come if you enjoy the rough and tumble of bargain hunting. As well as traders selling new goods, there are second-hand stalls full of bric-a-brac, records and antiques.

People's Palace

Glasgow Green. Tel: (0141) 554 0223. Open: Mon–Thur and Sat 1000–1700; Fri and Sun 1100–1700. Admission free.

Essentially this is a museum about Glasgow and the collection covers everything, from paintings and artefacts to oral history recordings and displays on the city's old 'steamies' – the **public wash houses**. It was purpose-built in 1898 as a 'palace of pleasure and imagination' for the working classes and combined the functions of art gallery, museum, winter garden and music hall. It was deliberately situated in the East End in order to be accessible to the poorest people in the city.

Exhibitions look at the different ethnic groups who have made Glasgow their home; life in the city during the two World Wars; and 'the patter', the distinctive Glaswegian dialect and way with words, which is frequently impenetrable to visitors. There is even an exhibition devoted to local indulgence in 'the bevvy' or alcoholic drink: displays include a barrow, used by police to carry drunks to jail, and an 18th-century punchbowl from an exclusive private drinking club.

Other rooms examine the city's history of manufacturing and trading and its socialist traditions. There are memorabilia from the women's suffrage movement, and a series of paintings by Ken Currie, depicting images from Glasgow's political history. Built on to the back of the museum is an enormous conservatory, The Winter Gardens, with tropical plants and a café.

Templeton's Carpet Factory

Glasgow Green.

This exotic confection of brick, mosaic and terracotta was designed by William Leiper in 1889. Purpose-built as a carpet factory, it was inspired by the Doge's Palace in Venice and is a vibrant landmark in a rather shabby part of the city. Only in Glasgow could such a lavish industrial building have been erected.

" *The world's finest example of decorative brickwork.* "

Architectural historian Frank Wordsall

Tolbooth Steeple

Glasgow Cross.

Taxi drivers take great pleasure in telling you that public hangings once took place here. The steeple, built in 1621, is all that remains of the old Tolbooth, a building that combined the functions of council offices, courthouse and jail. Seven storeys high, it stands at a busy junction, which was the hub of life in medieval Glasgow.

123

Old Glasgow

Glasgow Cathedral

Cathedral Square. Tel: (0141) 552 6891; www.historic-scotland.gov.uk.
Open: Apr–Sept, Mon–Sat 0930–1830, Sun 1400–1830; Oct–Mar,
Mon–Sat 0930–1630, Sun 1400–1630.

> " *Situated in a populous and considerable town, this ancient and massive pile has the appearance of the most sequestered solitude.* "

Sir Walter Scott on Glasgow Cathedral

For several centuries, Glasgow was the focal point of Christian culture in Scotland. A religious community was founded here in the 6th century by **St Mungo**, probably the first person to establish Christianity in the area. When he died, a church was built around his grave, parts of which can be seen in the cathedral crypt. The present, rather gloomy, cathedral was largely built between 1230 and 1330 and is unusual in having survived the Reformation.

Necropolis

Castle Street.

The Necropolis (meaning 'city of the dead') is a graveyard with a difference. High on a hilltop by the cathedral, this was where the great and the good – or the very wealthy – were buried. Most burials took place during the 19th century and the tombs and mausoleums are extremely elaborate. At the summit are monuments to **John Knox**, the father of the Reformation, and **William Miller**, the author of the nursery rhyme *Wee Willie Winkie*. Don't miss the monument to **Alexander McCall**, an ex-Chief Constable of Glasgow: a tall Celtic cross, it is the first documented solo work by none other than **Charles Rennie Mackintosh** and dates back to 1888.

Provand's Lordship

3 Castle Street. Tel: (0141) 553 2557. Closed for major structural repairs until the end of 2000.

This unassuming medieval building is the oldest house in Glasgow. It was once part of the cathedral precinct and was built in 1471 to house the chaplain of nearby St Nicholas's Hospital. For part of the 19th century it was used as an ale house, and in the first part of the 20th century as a sweet shop.

St Mungo Museum of Religious Life and Art

2 Castle Street. Tel: (0141) 553 2557. Open: Mon–Thur and Sat 1000–1700; Fri and Sun 1100–1700. Admission free.

> " *Medieval Glasgow, of which so little survives, derived its importance from its standing as an episcopal see. The city owes its origins to the impulses of religion.* "
>
> **Allan Massie, writer and journalist**

Disparagingly dubbed the 'Weetabix building' by local cabbies, this museum aims to reflect the importance of religion in human life and displays religious artefacts from around the world. There is a Hindu bronze of Shiva as Nataraja, and a Kalabari funerary screen from Nigeria, a memorial to a dead chief or ancestor. The best known work of art is the dramatic painting *Christ of St John of the Cross* by Salvador Dalí, which was inspired by a sketch drawn by a mystic Carmelite friar, who may have experienced a vision similar to this.

The Gallery of Religious Life looks at rites of passage, religious wars and death. Exhibits range from African initiation masks and Hindu bridal clothes, to a sword used during the Crusades. On the top floor is a gallery dealing with the thorny subject of religion in the west of Scotland. It examines the sectarian divide between Catholics and Protestants, as well as religions introduced more recently into Scotland such as Judaism, Hinduism and Islam. Behind the building is a Zen Garden. Its stark simplicity contrasts uneasily with the flamboyance of the Necropolis, which overlooks it.

125

The Merchant City

The Merchant City got its name from the wealthy merchants who lived and worked here from the mid-18th century. It was a planned development that took them away from the city slums around the High Street. Their imposing mansions, office premises and warehouses were built from the profits of trade with the Americas – trade that focused on the import of tobacco, rum and sugar.

These entrepreneurs, or Tobacco Lords as they were known, imported about half of all the tobacco that came into Britain and controlled most of Europe's tobacco trade. It was the wealth created by these merchants that funded Glasgow's expansion into heavy industry and textile manufacturing in the 19th century and also led to the city's growth westwards.

During the mid to late 20th century the area had fallen into disrepair but regeneration began in the 1980s and now it is one of the coolest and trendiest parts of the city. More and more of the Merchant City's grand old buildings are being converted. Stroll through the streets and discover its cool and quirky shops, and trendy bars and cafés.

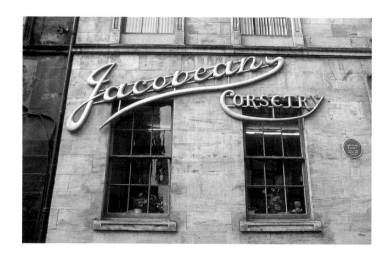

Hutchesons' Hall

158 Ingram Street. Tel: (0141) 552 8391; www.nts.org.uk. Open: Mon–Sat 1000–1700, except public holidays and 24 Dec–6 Jan. Admission free.

This Grade A listed building takes its name from the Hutcheson brothers, philanthropists who came from a wealthy land-owning family. They founded a hospital in 1639 to look after 'poor decrepit men' and educate orphaned boys. The hospital was moved to its present location in the early 19th century and was later changed to offices to administer the payment of pensions. You can see the ornate hall upstairs, while the ground floor has an information centre for the National Trust for Scotland and a gift shop.

Italian Centre

Ingram Street.

Created from the shell of abandoned old buildings, the Italian Centre, with its sculptures and statues, is a temple to Italian design and one of the most exclusive shopping centres in Glasgow. Wear your smartest clothes and set off to raid the racks of **Armani** (*10 John Street; tel: (0141) 552 2277*) and **Versace** (*162 Ingram Street; tel: (0141) 552 6510*), the first Versace store to open in Britain. When you've finished shopping, join the cool folk drinking creamy cappuccinos in the courtyard.

Trades Hall

85 Glassford Street. Tel: (0141) 552 2418. Open: Mon–Sat 0900–1800. Admission free.

Worth seeing as this is **Robert Adam**'s only surviving building in Glasgow. It was established as a meeting place and office for the city's incorporated trades, who enjoyed immense respect from the rest of the city in their day. Inside, the **Grand Hall** is panelled with Spanish mahogany and lined with a Belgian silk tapestry that depicts the work of the various trades. These ranged from skinners and cordiners (bootmakers) to bonnetmakers and barbers (who were also the surgeons of their time).

127

Eating and drinking

Bars and restaurants

Babbity Bowster
16–18 Blackfriars Street. Tel: (0141) 552 5055. £. This traditional bar is a favourite with Glaswegians. As well as drinks, it serves filling Franco-Scottish meals and tasty sandwiches.

Café Gandolfi
64 Albion Street. Tel: (0141) 552 6813. ££. This friendly, well-established bistro serves high-standard sandwiches, soups and meals with a Franco-Scottish flavour. The warm, wooden interior features **Tim Stead**'s trademark chunky furniture.

Cathedral House
28–32 Cathedral Square. Tel: (0141) 552 3519. ££. There's a medieval feel to this restaurant but, some would say luckily, the same does not apply to the food, which is contemporary Scottish cuisine.

City Merchant
97–9 Candleriggs. Tel: (0141) 553 1577. ££. Seafood is a speciality here. You can try everything, from Loch Etive mussels to langoustines and sea bass.

Corinthian
191 Ingram Street. Tel: (0141) 552 1101. ££. Originally a glorious old bank, topped with a huge glass dome, Corinthian has two separate bars as well as a bistro. Come here for cocktails in elegant surroundings.

Inn on the Green
23 Greenhead Street, Glasgow Green. Tel: (0141) 554 0165. £. Popular, well-established restaurant conveniently placed close to the People's Palace.

Scottische
16–18 Blackfriars Street. Tel: (0141) 552 7774. ££. Cosy restaurant at the heart of the Merchant City, located above the Babbity Bowster. Serves good-quality Scottish food. Dishes range from fish stew to roast venison.

Nightlife

Life
191 Ingram Street. Club at the Corinthian, converted from former jail cells. Music is funk and soul.

Coffee Stop

Toast
86 Albion Street. Tel: (0141) 552 3044. £. Buzzy, 21st-century café serving coffee, sandwiches and delicious things on toast such as flat field mushrooms and ricotta, or pastrami and Swiss cheese on ciabatta.

Shopping

As well as the Italian Centre, there are plenty of other stylish shops worth investigating in the Merchant City. Try **Cruise** *(* 180–8 Ingram Street *) for cool clothes and* **La Bottega di Mamma Ru** *(* Merchants' Square, Bell Street *) for fabrics and chunky church candles. Lovers of chic interior design should head for* **Inhouse** *(* 24–6 Wilson Street *), which stocks goods by renowned names such as* **Alessi and Philippe Starck**.

129

No Mean City

Few cities can have suffered from such a negative image as Glasgow. For years it was perceived as violent and filthy – a byword for squalor. Its original Gaelic name glas chu, *meaning 'dear green place', seemed like a rather bad joke. Writing in 1996, Lynn Cochrane remembered* The Scotsman's *columnist Albert Morris talking about the time he and his class were led up Arthur's Seat in Edinburgh. His teacher 'pointed to a smudge on the horizon. "That's where Glasgow lies," he told the class gravely. "It's a place you should try to avoid".'*

Glasgow was certainly once a filthy city, polluted by noxious gases and grime from its factories. And many people were certainly poor, particularly when its traditional heavy industries went into decline. Apparently around 90,000 people were crammed into slums in **Gorbals** in the 1930s. Not surprisingly, this led to degradation and violence, all of which was captured graphically in the novel *No Mean City* by A McArthur and H Kingsley Long, published in 1935.

But cities change and none more so than Glasgow. During the 1980s blackened buildings were carefully cleaned and were found to possess a striking beauty. Young professionals

GLASGOW – THE EAST END AND MERCHANT CITY

began to move into the renovated tenements and smart shops started to open up. The city regained its confidence and tourists began to discover its great museums, thriving arts scene and friendly people.

In 1990 Glasgow was selected as **European City of Culture**, and in 1999 it was named **UK City of Architecture**. People who come for the first time are surprised at how green it is, enjoying more than 70 parks, some with beautiful river walks and woodlands. At **Mugdock Country Park**, just ten miles from the city centre, you could be forgiven for thinking that you were deep in the heart of the countryside.

131

Of course, the problems of poverty and poor housing have not been eradicated in Glasgow. But then they have not been eradicated in Edinburgh, or London, Paris or Rome, Los Angles or New York. And you'd be hard pressed to find a more welcoming, innovative or stylish city than Scotland's 'dear green place'.

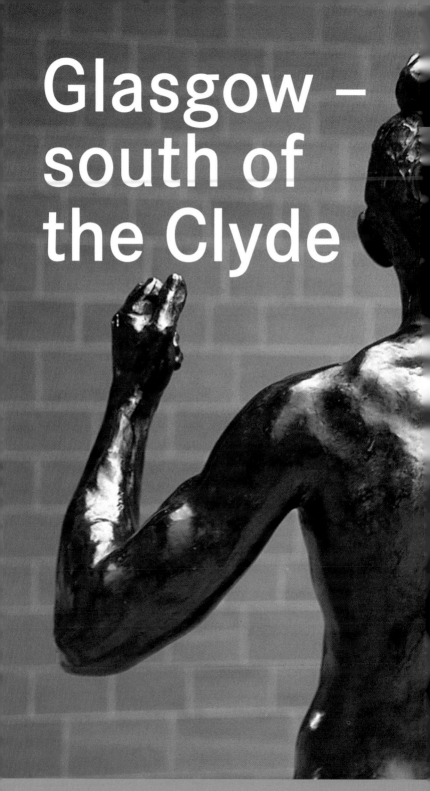

Glasgow – south of the Clyde

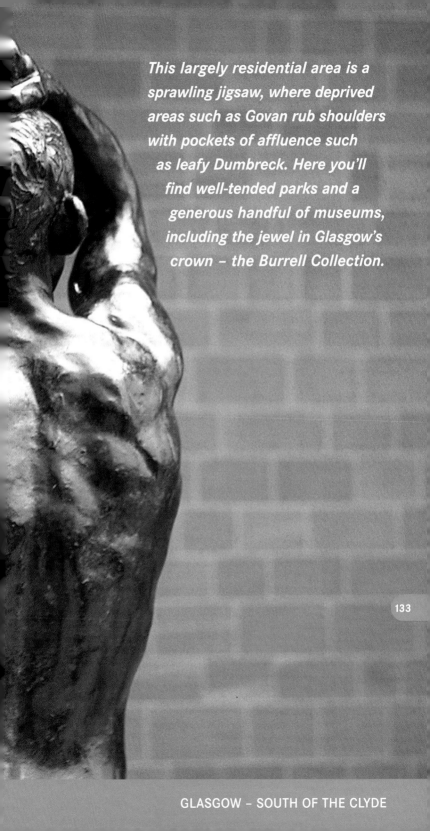

This largely residential area is a sprawling jigsaw, where deprived areas such as Govan rub shoulders with pockets of affluence such as leafy Dumbreck. Here you'll find well-tended parks and a generous handful of museums, including the jewel in Glasgow's crown – the Burrell Collection.

133

Glasgow – south of the Clyde

*Getting there: sites on the South Side are spread out a lot further and you might think of hiring a **taxi**. For Scotland Street School Museum, take the **underground** to Shields Road. For the Burrell Collection and Pollok House, get on the **train** to Pollokshaws Station, or catch **buses** 45 or 47 to Pollokshaws Road, then **walk** for about ten minutes. For Holmwood House, wait for bus 66, 44 or 44A/D to Clarkston Road, then walk. For House for an Art Lover, take buses 39, 50, 54, 55 or 56. For Govan Parish Church, catch buses 89 or 90.*

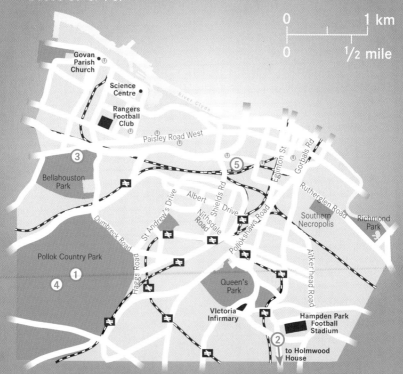

① *The Burrell Collection*

If you visit nothing else in Glasgow, visit the Burrell Collection. This varied and idiosyncratic collection of over 8,000 works of art was the lifetime collection of Sir William Burrell, a wealthy Glaswegian shipowner.
Pages 136–7

② *Holmwood House*

This elegant house is a reminder that Glasgow has produced more than one architect of note. It was designed and built by Alexander 'Greek' Thomson and is regarded as his finest house.
Page 139

③ *House for an Art Lover*

This innovative house was inspired by original designs by Glasgow's favourite architect, Charles Rennie Mackintosh. It has a country feeling, set in Bellahouston Park, beside a Victorian walled garden. **Page 139**

④ *Pollok House*

See how the other half once lived in this 18th-century mansion, the home of the local land-owning family, the Maxwells, who lived here until well into the 20th century. **Page 140**

⑤ *Scotland Street School Museum*

Memories of skinned knees and tickings-off from the teacher come flooding back as soon as you step into this airy, Mackintosh-designed school. It closed in 1979 and now contains reconstructed classrooms from different eras. **Page 141**

The Burrell Collection

2060 Pollokshaws Road, Pollok Country Park. Tel: (0141) 287 2550. Open:
Mon–Thur and Sat 1000–1700; Fri and Sun 1100–1700. Admission free.

It is difficult to imagine that the glorious works of art in this
collection were shut away in cupboards for almost forty years.
That, however, was the case, as it took years for the council
to find a suitable place in which to display them. When the
shipping magnate **Sir William Burrell** donated his entire
art collection to the city of Glasgow in 1944, he was concerned
about the threat of damage from industrial pollution. He
therefore stipulated that the works should be housed in one
building (for which he provided funding) in a rural setting,
not more than 16 miles from the Royal Exchange. It was not
until the **Clean Air Act** of the 1960s, coupled with council
acquisition of Pollok Park, that a suitable site was found.

> *Among the city's many treasures, none shines brighter, in my view, than the Burrell Collection.*

Bill Bryson, *Notes from a Small Island*

The building in which the collection is housed is light and airy, and many items from the stash of paintings have been cleverly incorporated into its fabric. You walk through medieval stone doorways, stare up at an ancient oak ceiling, and peep through stained-glass windows. The effect is to bring freshness and intimacy to the collection.

Burrell's interest in acquiring art began when he was a boy and he continued collecting until he died in 1958 at the age of 96. The collection reflects his personal taste and is particularly strong in late Gothic and early Renaissance works from northern Europe. The tapestries, which represent the most valuable part of the collection, mostly date from the late 15th and early 16th centuries. There is a vibrant work from **Tournai**, *Peasants Hunting Rabbits with Ferrets*, and a richly coloured 16th-century hanging, *The Camp of the Gypsies*. Among the medieval works, don't miss the stunning stained glass and religious reliquaries.

The great thing about the Burrell Collection is its variety; Sir William collected anything that took his fancy: lace, ceramics, carpets, silver, even Egyptian art. It is here that you'll find **Rodin**'s *Thinker*, which is far smaller than you might expect. And then there are the paintings that include **Giovanni Bellini**'s *Madonna with Child*, **Degas**' *Jockeys in the Rain* and **Eugene Boudin**'s atmospheric *The Empress Eugenie on the Beach at Trouville*. You should be aware that not all items in the collection can be displayed at once and so exhibits may change.

137

Govan Parish Church

Govan Road. Tel: (0141) 445 1941. Open: first Wed in June to third Saturday in Sept, Wed 1030–1230; Wed, Thur, Sat 1300–1600.

Govan may be the home of **Rab C Nesbitt**, but it also contains this 19th-century church, which stands on an ancient Christian site. It's not on the usual tourist trail, but worth visiting for its unique collection of carved stones, spanning the 9th to 11th centuries. Look for the elaborately carved cross-shafts, ornamented with mysterious figures and patterns and unusual humpback tombstones called 'hogbacks'. Rather prosaically, a sarcophagus, finely decorated with animals and interlaced ribbons, has a hole in the bottom, allowing drainage as the corpse decomposed. The church also features some vibrant and detailed stained-glass windows.

Holmwood House

61–3 Netherlee Road. Tel: (0141) 637 2129. Open: 1 Apr–31 Oct, daily 1330–1730. Access may be restricted at peak times. ££.

Thomas Gildard once wrote, 'If architecture be poetry in stone-and-lime … this exquisite little gem, at once classic and picturesque, is as complete, self contained, and polished as a sonnet'. Holmwood is a bit further from the city centre than other attractions, but is well worth the effort if you're interested in fine houses. Despite his name, **Alexander 'Greek' Thomson** never actually went to Greece, yet he believed that the architecture of the Ancient Greeks provided the ideal basis for modern design. The villa was built in the Classical Greek style for the owner of a local paper mill and Thomson was given great freedom over the design. The interior is light and spacious and the walls are richly decorated with classically inspired patterns.

House for an Art Lover

10 Dumbreck Road, Bellahouston Park. Tel: (0141) 353 4770;
www.houseforanartlover.co.uk. Call for opening times. ££.

Despite its appearance, this house was only built in the 1990s
following a 1901 design by Charles Rennie Mackintosh.
He had prepared the drawings as an entry for an international
competition for a 'House for an Art Lover'. He received a
special prize for the originality of his design, and his plans
helped to establish his reputation as an architect. His wife,
Margaret Macdonald, also had an important input into
the work.

Pollok House

2060 Pollokshaws Road, Pollok Country Park. Tel: (0141) 616 6410. Open:
1 Apr–31 Oct, daily 1000–1700; 1 Nov–31 Mar, daily (except 25–6 Dec and
1–2 Jan) 1100–1600. ££.

Set amid lush and leafy Pollok Park, and conveniently close
to the Burrell Collection, Pollok House is a grand Georgian
country house. Its former owners, the
Maxwell family, had been established at
Pollok from the mid-13th century and
owned most of southern Glasgow. This
house replaced earlier castles and was
designed by **William Adam** in around
1740. The building is sleek and austere, and looks out across
a fine parterre and immaculately clipped lawns.

> " *The Clyde almost runs*
> *through my veins.* "
>
> **Billy Connolly**

The interiors are as grand as you would expect of any stately
home and house a good collection of Spanish works of art.
These include *Lady in a Fur Wrap* and *Portrait of a Man* by
El Greco and pieces by **Goya** and **Murillo**. Most people's
favourite parts of the house are the servants' quarters,
which offer a fascinating insight into life 'below stairs'.
There are rows of bells that might ring from any part of
the house, tiled corridors and an enormous kitchen with
an original cast-iron range.

Science Centre

Pacific Quay. Tel: (0141) 420 5000. Open: the cinema will open in Autumn
2000, the rest of the site by Spring 2001.

The most exciting development on the south bank of the Clyde
is Glasgow's £75-million Science Centre. Sited practically
opposite the Scottish Exhibition and Conference Centre, this
futuristic development will bring science and technology alive.
In the main **Exhibits Building** there will be a planetarium,
a laboratory and experiment areas, while a 100-m **Wing
Tower** will give panoramic views across the city. It will also
be the location for Scotland's first **IMAX 3D cinema**.

Scotland Street School Museum

225 Scotland Street. Tel: (0141) 287 0500. Open: Mon–Thur and Sat 1000–1700; Fri and Sun 1100–1700. Admission free.

Charles Rennie Mackintosh seriously blew his budget when he built this school for the School Board in 1906. It's an enormous, airy building with lots of gleaming tiles and a strong hint of floor polish, which generally transports people straight back to their schooldays. It's a great place to bring children as they are fascinated by the classrooms that have been restored to represent the teaching regimes of various eras. The Victorian–Edwardian Classroom has tiered rows of desks and a distinct air of severity. The Second World War Classroom has slates on the desks, as well as gas masks, which had to be kept handy in case of an air raid. There is also a 1950s–1960s Classroom and an exhibition of aspects of Scottish education over the years. Local schools come here to re-enact Victorian lessons, often shocking the children into silence.

Eating and drinking

As the south side of the river is largely residential, there aren't nearly as many restaurants as in the city centre. However, that doesn't mean that it is a culinary black hole. The restaurants here cater to a loyal following of locals and offer good food at reasonable prices.

Restaurants

Ashoka Southside
268 Clarkston Road. Tel: (0141) 637 0711. ££. One of a chain of reliable Indian restaurants in Glasgow.

The Battlefield Rest
55 Battlefield Road. Tel: (0141) 636 6955. £. You'll need to book ahead at this popular Italian restaurant. It not only offers pizzas, but also some unusual dishes such as sweet pickled herrings with orange and beetroot.

Buongiorno
1012 Pollokshaws Road. Tel: (0141) 649 1029. £. Creating excellent and authentic Italian food, this place is said to serve the best pizzas in Glasgow.

Cul-de-Sac Southside
1179 Pollokshaws Road. Tel: (0141) 649 1819. ££. Popular with couples, this restaurant is the sister to Cul-de-Sac in the West End. The food is French and includes a good selection of crêpes.

The Greek Golden Kebab
34 Sinclair Drive, Battlefield. Tel: (0141) 649 7581. £–££. Booking essential for Fri and Sat nights. Despite its name, this isn't a takeaway but a family-run Greek restaurant. Try a four-course *meze*, lamb on the bone or one of several vegetarian options.

Russell's
219 Fenwick Road, Giffnock. Tel: (0141) 620 1003. ££. A bit out of the way but worth the journey. This is a cosy bistro serving main courses such as Aberdeen Angus steaks. A good-value lunch menu changes daily.

Shimla Pinks
777 Pollokshaws Road. Tel: (0141) 423 4488. ££. Cool, chrome, designer, Indian restaurant. The food is fresh and includes some house specialities such as Assamese chicken jalfreizi.

The Wok Way
2 Burnfield Road, Giffnock. Tel: (0141) 638 2244. ££. Don't make the journey out here unless you've booked. This Chinese restaurant is not only small, but extremely popular (there's even karaoke at weekends). Highlights include sea bass with ginger and spring onions.

Cafés

South-side cafés tend towards the traditional egg and beans, or tea and pastries, variety but there are a few places where you can find a good coffee or a snack.

Café Blankitt
378 Cathcart Road. Tel: (0141) 423 5172. £–££. Comfy sofas in the lounge, adventurous sandwiches and bagels in the café. Meals are served in the evening and include dishes such as hot camembert.

There are also good cafés at the **Burrell Collection** and at **House for an Art Lover.**

Nightlife

Theatres
The south side is home to one of Britain's most influential theatres, **The Citizens'** (*Gorbals Street; tel: (0141) 429 0022*). Superb auditorium and an adventurous programme of performances.

There is also **The Tramway** (*25 Albert Drive; tel: (0141) 422 2023*).

PROFILE

The amber nectar

There can be few countries that have a more famous national drink than Scotland. Whisky is sold all over the

world and monthly sales in France exceed those of cognac. Yet despite popular perception, whisky has not always been Scotland's favourite drink; for centuries people preferred to drink ale – and claret.

> " *Leith bottled claret held in its day a cachet comparable to that which one now associates with Chateau bottled wines.* "
>
> **J G Thomson, historian**

Wine was introduced to Scotland by the Romans in the 1st century AD. It was the everyday drink of the Legions and their main supply depot was at Leith in Edinburgh, which soon grew into a significant wine port. Trading links with the continent ensured that claret, together with locally brewed beer and ale, became Scotland's staple beverage.

Claret drinking only really declined in the 19th century: taxes made it more expensive; the Napoleonic wars meant that supplies were hard to come by; and the quality declined when French vines were devastated by diseases. People began to drink spirits instead, as these were now cheaper than ever. While the English acquired a taste for gin, the Scots turned to whisky, rapidly increasing its popularity.

The word 'whisky' comes from the Gaelic *uisge beatha*, meaning 'water of life'. This was shortened to *uisge*, pronounced *oosky*, which eventually became 'whisky'. The tale goes that it was brought to Scotland during the 5th century by the Scotti, the invaders from Ireland who gave their name to the country.

Distillation was first recorded in Scotland in the 15th century. There are two types of Scotch whisky: malt whisky, made from malted barley, wheat and yeast; and grain whisky, made from a mash of cereals, rather than barley alone. Blended whisky is a combination of the two. There are around one hundred distilleries in Scotland and the whiskies produced reflect the land and climate in which they are made: some are peaty, others smoky, some peppery, others smooth.

As well as tasting whisky, make sure you try Scottish beers, which tend to be sweeter than those from England. Look out too for Scotland's amber-coloured soft drink, Irn Bru. Created in Glasgow in 1901, it is made following a closely guarded secret recipe and is a popular hangover cure.

Further afield – walks and excursions

Edinburgh and Glasgow both make excellent bases for exploring the beautiful Scottish countryside. Plenty of places worth visiting are just an hour or so away. You can even bring your walking boots and stride out across the hills.

147

Dalmeny and South Queensferry I

You could easily spend the day out here, as there is lots to see – and it's only a 15-minute train journey from the centre of Edinburgh. South Queensferry takes its name from the first ferry across the Firth of Forth, which was established here in the 11th century by Queen Margaret to aid pilgrims travelling to Dunfermline. The service continued until 1964, when the New Road Bridge opened. The town's esplanade is the place to view the great Forth bridges – road and rail – that link Edinburgh and the south with Fife.

Dalmeny House

South Queensferry. Tel: (0131) 331 1888. Open: July and Aug, Mon and Tues 1200–1730, Sun 1300–1730. ££.

Standing at the western end of South Queensferry, this is the home of the **Earl of Rosebery**, who owns practically all the land you can see in this area. The house is stuffed with French furniture, beautiful paintings, porcelain and tapestries (designed by **Goya**). There are pleasant walks through the lovely grounds and along the shore of the Forth.

Forth Railway Bridge

The cantilevered Forth Railway Bridge was such an achievement that it is considered to be the Victorian equivalent of the landing on the moon. Just a few years before it was built, the **Tay Bridge** had been blown down in a gale, killing 75 people, so an enormous amount of work

Tourist information

Forth Bridges Tourist Information Centre, near North Queensferry, tel: 01383 417 759; open all year.

> " I think it's the nicest looking bridge in the whole world. It is Scotland's Eiffel Tower. "
>
> **Billy Connolly on the Forth Railway Bridge**

was put into its design. Completed in 1890, it is 1.5 miles (2.4km) long and took seven years to build; 57 workers were killed during its construction. A visitor centre on the north bank (follow signs to the tourist information centre off the approach to the road bridge) tells the fascinating story of its construction.

The phrase 'painting the Forth Bridge' has become synonymous with a task that is never finished, and you are almost certain to see maintenance crews at work. Some tasks are tackled by skilled abseilers. Just by the bridge is the Hawes Inn, an ancient inn where Robert Louis Stevenson wrote *Kidnapped*.

Getting there: you can take First Edinburgh bus 43 from the bus station to South Queensferry. It stops near Dalmeny House. Trains run regularly from Waverley and Haymarket stations to Dalmeny. From there it is a ten-minute walk down to the Forth Railway Bridge. To get to Hopetoun House you really need a car as it is quite a walk from a bus stop, and even further from the station – otherwise take a taxi.

Dalmeny and South Queensferry II

Hopetoun House

South Queensferry. Tel: (0131) 331 2451. Open: Easter–end Sept, Mon–Sun 1000–1730; weekends in October. ££.

This opulent pile, situated in 100 acres (25 hectares) of parkland along the shores of the Firth of Forth at South Queensferry, is the family home of the earls and marquises of **Linlithgow**. Hopetoun House is the work of two outstanding Scottish architects. The original building, designed by Sir William Bruce in classical style and

constructed between 1699 and 1707, is adorned with superb carving, wainscoting and ceiling painting. In 1721 the house was enlarged by the architect William Adam, who added the handsome façade, colonnades, ballroom and state apartments. Hopetoun House is stuffed with treasures and fine furnishings that reflect the elegant lifestyle of the 18th-century Scottish aristocracy. George IV's visit to Hopetoun House in 1822 prompted the revival of Highland dress and an interest in Scottish traditions. There are fine views from the rooftop terrace, while the grounds contain a Spring Garden, a Red Deer Park and several picnic spots. The grounds also have woodlands, which are filled with primroses and bluebells in spring, and there are magnificent views to be had of the Forth bridges.

Maid of the Forth

Hawes Pier. Tel: (0131) 331 4857. Open: Easter–Oct. Call for sailing times. ££.

Maid of the Forth cruises under the Forth Railway Bridge and on to Inchcolm Island, where there's a ruined 12th-century abbey. You have a good chance of spotting seals, puffins and even dolphins. The *Maid* also does evening cruises in summer with live jazz or a traditional *ceilidh*.

Queensferry Museum

High Street. Tel: (0131) 331 5545. Open: Mon–Sat 1000–1300, then 1415–1700, and Sun 1200–1700. Admission free.

This interesting little museum contains displays relating to the Forth Railway Bridge, as well as a model of the Burry Man. Every year a local man is covered in a suit of sticky burrs, decorated with flowers and led around the town's boundaries, preceded by someone ringing a bell. His origins are almost certainly pagan.

Haddington

Getting there: First Edinburgh **bus** *106 runs to Haddington from Princes Street. If you want to go to Lennoxlove you will then need to get a* **taxi**.

This rather staid but attractive town is an easy trip from Edinburgh. It was laid out in the 12th century, although most of the buildings that you see date from the 17th to the 19th centuries. Haddington is said to be the birthplace of John Knox, the 16th-century religious reformer who founded the Presbyterian movement and led the attack on the Catholic Church in Scotland.

One of the loveliest parts of the town is just outside the centre, by the River Tyne. You can stroll along the river, feed the swans or sit outside at the Waterside Bistro – a popular place for Sunday lunch. This part of the river is dominated by St Mary's Church, which dates back to the 15th century.

Lennoxlove House

Haddington. Tel: (01620) 823720. Open: Easter–end Oct, Wed and Thur, some Sats and Sun 1400–1630. Guided tours available. ££.

Lennoxlove dates back to the 14th century and is the home of the Duke of Hamilton. The house was originally called 'Lethington', and took its current name from Frances Teresa Stewart, Duchess of Richmond and Lennox. She was a maid of honour at the court of Charles II, and her beauty made her a great favourite with the king, who showered her with presents. One of these, an inlaid tortoiseshell writing cabinet, is on display in the house today.

The house also contains interesting mementoes of Mary, Queen of Scots, including a silver casket that played an important role in her eventual downfall. Her accusers produced the casket, claiming that it contained letters implicating her in the murder of her second husband, Lord Darnley. It is now thought that they were forgeries.

153

New Lanark World Heritage Village

Getting there: hire a car or take a train from Glasgow Central to Lanark and then a bus to New Lanark. For more information, telephone the Visitor Centre on (01555) 661345 (open: daily 1100–1700); www.newlanark.org. ££.

This World Heritage Site is something really different. New Lanark was built around 1785 by David Dale as a new industrial settlement. He wanted to exploit the power of the spectacular Falls of Clyde in order to run lucrative cotton mills. Housing was built for the workforce and by 1820 it was one of the largest cotton manufacturing centres in the country.

Dale's son-in-law Robert Owen managed the village from 1820 to 1825 and set about making it the location for an ambitious social experiment. In an era when working people were routinely exploited by industrialists, Owen abolished the practice of employing pauper apprentices and phased out the use of child labour (no child under 10 was allowed to work in the mills).

> What ideas individuals may attach to the term 'Millennium' I know not; but I know that society may be formed so as to exist without crime, without poverty ... and with intelligence and happiness increased a hundredfold.

Robert Owen speaking to the inhabitants of New Lanark

Owen's idea was to create a social environment in which man's character could be improved. He set up a co-operative store, the profits of which were ploughed back into education, and an Institute for the Formation of Character. This contained a library and reading room and became the social centre of the village. Villagers also received free medical care. There was great emphasis on education and Owen established the first infant school in the world. As part of this revolutionary step, the children were not punished and were taught a wide curriculum, including music, art, nature studies, history and geography – as well as the three basic 'Rs'.

New Lanark today is full of atmosphere. Many people still live in the restored buildings, so you cannot see inside them. However, a millworker's house has been restored, showing living conditions from the 1820s and 1930s. The Village Store has been refurbished and there is an exhibition about Robert Owen in his old house.

You can see the machinery inside the mill, which has an eerie appeal, as though the workers had just left their posts. This might have been Owen's idea of Utopia, but life was still hard. Labourers had to work for 12 hours a day, six days a week, and there was a so-called 'silent monitor' system. This was the practice of suspending a painted block of wood above each worker's head. The colour denoted whether they had been good or bad that day – and whippings could be issued as punishment.

New Lanark's a great place for children as well as adults. They'll particularly enjoy the 'dark ride' journey through time. The village is set in a beautiful spot and there are plenty of walks through the Falls of Clyde Wildlife Reserve. The waterfall has a picturesque appeal and you may even spot kingfishers on the river.

If you really want to soak up the atmosphere, you can stay at New Lanark Mill Hotel (*tel: (01555) 667200*), a converted cotton mill. There is also self-catering accommodation in The Waterhouses.

155

Peebles

*Getting there: First Edinburgh **bus** 62 runs from the bus station to Peebles and then goes to Innerleithen. If you want to visit Traquair House you will need to get a **taxi** from Peebles or Innerleithen. Phone Peebles **Tourist Office** for detailed information (High Street; tel: (01721) 720138; open: all year).*

A trip to Peebles gives you a taste of the Borders, yet it is only about an hour from Edinburgh. There are some lovely walks that are accessible from the town centre, one of the easiest being along the River Tweed to 15th-century Neidpath Castle.

Peebles is a pleasant border town making a popular base for walkers and those wishing to fish for salmon on the River Tweed. Among its historical sites are the ruins of Cross Kirk, which was built by Alexander II in 1261. The town was the birthplace of the Chambers brothers, who published the first Chambers dictionaries and encyclopaedias.

Neidpath Castle

Peebles, Tweeddale. Tel: (01721) 720333. Open: Easter–1 May and 1 July–3 Sept, Mon–Sat 1100–1700, Sun 1300–1700. £.

There is little left of Neidpath Castle, although it looks stunning, set as it is right by the River Tweed. There is not a great deal to see inside. The castle dates back to the 15th century and had 11-ft (3-m) thick walls. It was badly damaged by Cromwell's forces and was later restored and sold to the Queensberry family.

Traquair House

Innerleithen, near Peebles. Tel: (01896) 830323; www.traquair.co.uk. Open: Apr–end Oct. ££.

This is a stately home with the emphasis firmly on the 'home'. Traquair dates back to the 10th century, although much of it was rebuilt in the 17th century. The present owners are the Maxwell-Stuarts, who have lived here since the 15th century. It is full of atmosphere, with little turrets and tiny windows.

The family's strong Catholic principles led to their deep involvement in the Jacobite movement. A previous earl was imprisoned in the Tower of London under sentence of death for his support of Bonnie Prince Charlie. He managed to escape from the Tower dressed as a maid and you can still see the cloak he wore.

As well as relics from the era of Mary, Queen of Scots and some fascinating Jacobite memorabilia, the house has a priest hole and a staircase that served as an escape route for persecuted Catholics. Outside are the famous Bear Gates or *Steekit Yetts*. Apparently they were closed during the Jacobite rising of 1745, when the family swore that they would never be opened until there was a Stuart king back on the throne. The house possesses its own brewery, where a potent ale, Traquair Ale, is made.

Roslin

*Getting there: to get to Rosslyn Chapel, catch First Edinburgh **bus** C70 from Princes Street, then 315 from the bus station. You will have about a ten-minute **walk** when you get there.*

Rosslyn Chapel

Roslin, Midlothian. Tel: (0131) 440 2159; www.rosslynchapel.org.uk. Open: Mon–Sat 1000–1700; Sun 1200–1645. ££.

Rosslyn Chapel is a fascinating place to visit and is filled with history, religion and superstition. It was built in 1446 by **William St Clair** of neighbouring Roslin Castle.

The Chapel has strong links with the mysterious **Knights Templar**, a medieval order of warrior monks originally formed to protect pilgrims travelling to the Holy Land after the First Crusade. One of the founder's wives was **Catherine de St Clair of Roslin**. During the 12th and 13th centuries, the Templars became immensely wealthy and powerful, owning property and acting as international bankers and financiers. They eventually became too dominant, however, and were persecuted, being accused of pagan idolatry and immorality. Many Templars took refuge in Scotland, reportedly taking many of their treasures – and secrets – with them.

Rosslyn Chapel is said to have been built as a memorial to the Templars and many believe that their treasures are hidden inside the building. Archaeologists are keen to excavate the vaults, which they think may contain ancient scrolls from Jerusalem, religious artefacts and jewels.

The Chapel is full of extraordinary carvings, including more than one hundred effigies of the Green Man. This is a pagan figure, said by some to symbolise the capacity for great goodness and great evil. The most famous carving in the Chapel is the exquisitely intricate Apprentice Pillar, standing next to a less elaborate pillar by the Master Mason. Legend has it that the mason was instructed to create a pillar so detailed that he did not dare to tackle the work until he had been to Rome for inspiration. In his absence his apprentice had a dream that he had finished the pillar himself. He set to work and carried out the design as it now stands. However, when the Master Mason returned he was so jealous that he killed the young man.

" *The stone both of the roof and walls is sculptured with leaves and flowers, so delicately wrought that I could have admired them for hours.* "

Dorothy Wordsworth on a visit to Rosslyn Chapel in 1807

Other carvings in the chapel depict a *danse macabre*, representing death's supremacy over mankind, and an angel playing the bagpipes. There is even corn or maize from the New World, which was unknown in Britain when the Chapel was built. It is possible that knowledge of the crops was given to the founder, William St Clair, by his grandfather, Prince Henry of Orkney. Henry is thought to have sailed from Orkney to Newfoundland and then to Nova Scotia in the 14th century, 100 years before Columbus. He is said to have wintered with the Micmac, a Native American tribe, who still pass on the legend that a great lord came from the east in a ship and taught them to fish with nets.

Rosslyn Glen

If you come to the Chapel it is worth taking a walk through nearby Rosslyn Glen. A favourite spot with Romantic painters and poets, such as J M W Turner and William and Dorothy Wordsworth, the glen has good paths and is lovely in spring when the bluebells are in bloom.

159

Other excursions from Glasgow

You're unlikely to want to escape from Glasgow as there's so much to see. But if you would like to get out of town and see a bit more of Scotland, you'll be amazed at how easy it is.

Canals

For nearly 200 years the **Forth and Clyde** and **Union Canals** were an important commercial transport link between Edinburgh and Glasgow. Although they eventually fell into disrepair, millions of pounds have recently been plunged into restoring these industrial waterways. A unique boat-lift is being constructed at Falkirk – the **Falkirk Wheel** – which will allow boats to sail between Edinburgh and Glasgow, and rowing and canoeing on the canals will be encouraged. You can already walk and cycle along stretches of the canals, and towpaths are being improved and restored all the time.

Tip

It's amazing how many people forget the most obvious excursion of all – visiting Glasgow if you're staying in Edinburgh, and vice versa. Trains run between the cities every 15 minutes, and the journey only lasts 50 minutes.

Glasgow's parks

The city's name derives from the Gaelic for 'dear green place', and you will be surprised at just how many parks there are around Glasgow. Some of those within the city are **Pollok Country Park** – where you'll find the Burrell Collection – **Bellahouston Park** and **Hogganfield Loch**. There is a huge recreation area at **Strathclyde Country Park** in Hamilton and you can also visit an **RSPB nature reserve** at Lochwinnoch (*tel: (01505) 842663*).

Tip

In spring you can see Great Crested Grebes performing their elaborate courtship display at Lochwinnoch.

Loch Lomond

Getting there: hire a car, *as public transport is not particularly frequent. Otherwise take a* train *from Queen Street to Balloch. You can then get a* bus *to Balmaha. You can also get a First Edinburgh bus (No 8) and change at Drymen for Balmaha.*

You tak' the High Road,
And I'll tak' the Low road,
And I'll be in Scotland afore ye.

The song is said to be about a Jacobite prisoner awaiting death and adds to the romance of this beautiful loch – the largest stretch of fresh water in Britain. The loch seems to combine all the best elements of Scotland's scenery: cool, crisp water, dramatic mountains, rich wildlife and – if you're lucky – an air of solitude.

The western bank of the loch has the clearest views – but it also has the busiest road, leading to the smart people's hotel Cameron House. If you want to go on a boat trip, head for the rather overdeveloped resorts of Balloch and Luss. The most atmospheric, but least accessible, part of the loch is on the east side. Heading out from Glasgow, you can stop at Drymen, a pretty village that seems more English than Scottish, with a pub, a green and a church (Billy Connolly once lived here). Continue up to Balmaha, where boats bob on the waterside and the fragrant smell of burning peat rises from nearby cottages. To go further up the loch you will have to walk along its slippery and rocky edges. Otherwise just relax and enjoy the scenery.

Waverley Paddle Steamer

Tel: (0141) 243 2224. (See page 107 for more information.) *££.*

During the summer months you can join this historic paddle steamer, just minutes from Glasgow city centre, and sail to destinations along the Clyde. Trips go to the lovely islands of Arran, Dunoon, Rothesay and the Kyles of Bute.

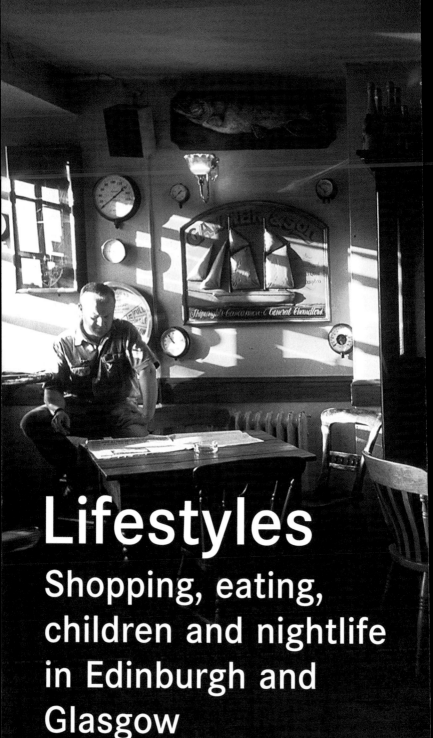

Lifestyles
Shopping, eating,
children and nightlife
in Edinburgh and
Glasgow

STAR

LIFESTYLES

Shopping

You can shop till you drop in both Glasgow and Edinburgh. As well as the well-known stores that you can find on any High Street, both cities also have plenty of designer-clothes stores. Glasgow has traditionally been the best city for clothes shopping, but Edinburgh is catching up fast.

The thriving tourist industry means that you will have plenty of opportunities to buy **traditional Scottish goods**. Whether you're after a kilt, a haggis, some whisky or a tin of shortbread, you will be able to find it somewhere.

There are also plenty of shops selling Scotland's high-quality **knitwear**. Look out too for **arts and crafts** by Scottish designers: pottery, jewellery and stained glass are all available in specialist shops.

Arts and crafts

You will easily be able to find places selling well-known brands such as **Edinburgh Crystal** and **Caithness Glass**, but you should also keep an eye out for locally made pottery, ceramics and lovely stained glass. There are also many **Rennie Mackintosh**-influenced goods, ranging from bookmarks to lamps. Try shops such as **Illumini** (*George IV Bridge*) and **Flux** (*Bernard Street*) in Edinburgh; **Glasgow**

Browsing

If you are looking for antiques at bargain prices you are sure to be disappointed. There are plenty of antique shops, auction rooms and bric-a-brac stores, but prices tend to be average or above (your best bet for a real bargain is probably a charity shop or **the Barras** in Glasgow). However, both cities have some great shops where you can find **retro jewellery** and clothing. There are good outlets in Edinburgh's **Grassmarket**, **Victoria Street** and **St Stephen Street**. Similar stores in Glasgow can be found around the **West End**, as well as **Victorian Village** in West Regent Street.

School of Art shop (*Renfrew Street*) and **Drooko** (*St Vincent Place*) in Glasgow.

Scottish jewellery generally has a delicate Celtic look, or is designed à la Rennie Mackintosh. You may also see traditional **luckenbooths**, rings given as love tokens, as well as **quaichs**, shallow cups used to drink a toast. In Glasgow try **Henderson** (*Sauchiehall Street*) or **Orro Contemporary Jewellery** (*Bank Street*). If you're in Edinburgh try **Scottish Gems** or **The Tappit Hen** (*both on the High Street*).

Clothes

Designer-clothes stores abound. In **Glasgow** head for the **Italian Centre** (home of Versace and Armani), **Ingram Street**, in the Merchant City, or **Princes Square** in Buchanan Street. **Edinburgh** has many designer outlets along **George Street** and will soon be getting Harvey Nichols as well. You can also find classic clothes at **Burberry**, in both Glasgow and Edinburgh, while established department stores are **Jenners** in Edinburgh and **Frasers** in Glasgow.

Scottish knitwear can be a good buy. There are lots of mill shops selling chunky Arran knits, and some excellent outlets selling quality cashmere. You can also find unusual designer knitwear at outlets such as Ragamuffin in Edinburgh's Royal Mile.

If you are determined to buy a kilt you will find a number of specialist shops where you can get them made to measure. Bear in mind that they will certainly not be cheap; you may prefer to restrict your tartan purchases to scarves or rugs.

Drink

Whisky is the one everyone wants and there is no shortage here – your only problem is likely to be trying to decide which kind to buy. Do you want a blended whisky or a malt whisky? A 10- or a 12-year-old malt? Do you want it smoky – like Laphroaig – or peppery like Talisker? The best thing is to go into a specialist shop (there are loads of them around) and ask the proprietor for some advice. If you're really keen you could join the Scotch Malt Whisky Society (tel: (0131) 555 2929), which holds tastings, provides information on malt whisky and gives members access to fine malts from all over Scotland.

Don't forget Scotland's other traditional drinks. You should be able to find Port of Leith port and claret, as well as that traditional liqueur Drambuie.

Food

As soon as you mention Scottish food, most people think of haggis. You can buy haggis in supermarkets, but the most famous one of all is made by Macsween of Edinburgh, who even make a vegetarian version. You can buy Macsween's haggis in Edinburgh at Peckhams in Bruntsfield Place or at Jenners.

Other Scottish foods which are widely available are smoked salmon, local cheeses (head for Ian Mellis in Victoria Street, Edinburgh), shortbread (Jenners in Edinburgh stock some good brands) and tablet, an extraordinarily sweet and crumbly type of fudge. Also look out for Brodies' chocolates, which have distinctively Scottish fillings such as whisky truffle.

Souvenirs

Souvenirs are widely available (Edinburgh's Royal Mile is probably the richest hunting ground) and can err towards the tacky. Look out for 'See you Jimmy' tartan hats complete with wild orange hair (as worn by Scottish football fans), fake bagpipes, Scottie dogs, models of Greyfriars Bobby and Loch Ness monsters, *Braveheart*-style costumes and dolls swathed in tartan.

If you are interested in exploring your Scottish ancestry there are shops that will take your name and then tell you exactly which tartan you should be wearing. It does not matter what your name is – they seem to be able to discover a tartan for anyone.

Other souvenirs that won't take up much room in your suitcase include tins of shortbread, Scottish jewellery and tartan scarves.

Eating out

Hardly a day goes by without a new restaurant, bar or bistro opening in Edinburgh and Glasgow. The inhabitants of both cities now eat out on a regular basis and you can find high-quality food available in simple bistros, as well as in restaurants run by celebrity chefs. Lots of style bars have also opened up, and you can enjoy light meals with an international flavour until late at night. The Scots do not, as some would have you believe, eat haggis every day and it is perfectly possible to dine your way around the world without leaving Scotland. Whether you fancy Moroccan, Russian, Swiss or Caribbean food you will be able to find it here. Vegetarians are also well catered for.

There was a time when Scottish food was seen to consist of little more than thick soups, haggis (sheep offal chopped up with oatmeal and onion) served with 'neeps' (swede) and potatoes, or mince and potatoes. But in recent years a modern style of Scottish cooking has emerged. Traditional dishes have been

given a contemporary twist and fresh, local produce has been utilised to create light, innovative dishes. **Haggis** may be served as a light starter with a piquant dressing, or appear inside a filo parcel; **Scotch beef** may be braised in a red wine sauce; **salmon** may be cooked in Darjeeling tea, and local **lamb** might be served with a pear compote. **Venison** appears on many menus and fresh **Scottish seafood**, noted for its quality, is a speciality of many restaurants. You can find Loch Etive mussels, monkfish, scallops, halibut, sea bass and herring.

Eating out is so popular now that it is often very difficult to get a table. You are always advised to book in advance, particularly for Friday and Saturday nights and during the Edinburgh Festival.

Eating times

Plenty of places serve food from early on. However, lunch is generally eaten between 1200 and 1400, and dinner between 1900 and 2200. **Pre-theatre** meals are commonly served and many places stay open until late at night. During the **Edinburgh Festival** many places in the city centre stay open round the clock.

Café society

Although Glasgow and Edinburgh may not have the sort of climate that encourages you to sit outside and sip your morning coffee, a lively **café culture** has built up in both cities. Generally open from early in the morning until late at night, these are relaxed places where you can come to read the paper, drink frothy cappuccinos or eat a snack. More substantial meals are frequently on offer and the best cafés attract a wide mix of people from students to lawyers.

Drinks

Whisky is the drink that everyone associates with Scotland and there are many pubs and bars offering a wide selection. Whisky is a complex drink and can be an acquired taste. Even if you don't like one brand, it doesn't mean that you won't enjoy another.

Spirits in Scotland were traditionally served in larger measures than in England (1/5 gill or even 1/4 gill, compared to the English 1/6 gill). However, measures have now been standardised and the usual measure is 25ml, as in England. That said, some pubs still serve a larger measure of 35ml, replacing the 1/4 gill.

PATISSERIE
FLORENTIN

Fast food

If you're on a tight budget or in a hurry, you don't have to go hungry. There are loads of fast food outlets selling burgers and takeaway pizzas, as well as sandwich bars that serve hungry office workers. There is also the original Scottish fast food – the fish supper (fish and chips) – which can be excellent. In Glasgow it's generally splashed with vinegar, in Edinburgh with brown sauce. Much has been made of the Scottish love of deep-fried food, and you will certainly see people eating battered black puddings and deep-fried pizzas – although the notorious deep-fried Mars bar is not much in evidence.

Don't forget Scottish beer. Edinburgh, in particular, has a long history as a brewing city, partly due to the range and quality of its water. Scottish beer tends to be sweeter than English beer. Ones to look out for include Deuchars, Golden Promise and Edinburgh Strong Ale.

Although you can get bottled water anywhere, there is really no need. The tap water has none of the chemical aftertaste you often find in big cities and tastes just as good as bottled varieties.

McSPORRANS

FEATHER FOWLIE
An Old Scots Chicken Soup
HAGGIS WI' TATTIES AN' NEEPS
Traditional But-Ben Recipe
ABERDEEN ANGUS STEAK SANDWICH
With Mushrooms, Onion & Horseradish Sauce
VENISON BURGER & REDCURRANT JELLY
Made with Ground Wild Venison
HIGHLANDER BURGER WITH ONIONS
Made with Prime Angus Beef
LARGE SCOTDOG WITH ARRAN MUSTARD
Inverness Pork Sausage Meat & Wild Herbs
CHIPS THICK CUT
Made with Scots Tatties
TEA, COFFEE, HOT CHOC, BOVRIL,
SOFT DRINKS

Pub debates are to Glasgow, what the forum was in Roman times.

Jimmy Reid, trade union activist, journalist and broadcaster.

Round the world

Scotland's 'auld alliance' with France
has left a culinary legacy. There are
plenty of French restaurants and
bistros in Glasgow and Edinburgh,
as well as places that offer Franco-
Scottish cuisine.

Both Glasgow and Edinburgh also
have established Italian communities,
and there are numerous places
serving delicious – and authentic –
Italian food. The cities' Asian
communities have also made their
mark – to such an extent that
Glasgow was once dubbed 'the
curry capital of Europe'. Along with
'British-Indian' dishes such as the
ubiquitous chicken tikka massala,
you will find sauces made with
almonds and saffron, spicy chickpeas
with pomegranate seeds, tandoori
smoked salmon and fragrant rice.

171

Edinburgh and Glasgow with children

Have no fear: there is a multitude of activities that will keep all ages quiet, from tiny tots to eternal Peter Pans.

Edinburgh

Bo'ness and Kinneil Railway

Bo'ness Station, Union Street, Bo'ness. Tel: (01506) 822298. Open: 14 Mar– 17 Oct, daily except Mon in July and Aug. ££. Restored railway station and steam trains. You can take a trip on a steam train out into the countryside.

Deep Sea World

North Queensferry, Fife. Tel: (01383) 411880; www.deepseaworld.com. Open: Mon–Sun 1000–1800 (1830 in Jul and Aug); closes at 1700 Nov–Mar. ££. Just over the Forth Railway Bridge this enormous, award-winning aquarium has piranhas, conger eels and lots more.

Dynamic Earth

(See page 27.)

Edinburgh Butterfly and Insect World

Lasswade, Midlothian. Tel: (0131) 663 4932. Open: 1000–1700 in winter; 0930–1730 in summer. ££. Exotic butterflies in a tropical rainforest setting – also regular insect-handling sessions.

Museum of Childhood

42 High Street, Royal Mile. Tel: (0131) 529 4142. Open: Mon–Sat 1000– 1700; also Sun during the Festival 1400–1700. Admission free. The world's first museum on this theme, reputedly created by a man who disliked children and dedicated it to King Herod. Full of old toys, teddy bears and train sets.

Museum of Flight

East Fortune Airfield, near Haddington. Tel: (01620) 880308; www.nms.ac/flight. Open: Mon–Sun 1030–1700. £; children free. A great place to bring would-be pilots, this is Scotland's National Museum of Aviation, with a huge collection of historic aircraft.

Glasgow

Science Centre
(See page 141.)

Football Clubs

Young football fanatics should easily be bribed with the promise of visits to Glasgow's famous football clubs. Celtic Football Club Visitor Centre (*Celtic Park; tel: (0141) 551 4308; www.celticfc.co.uk; open: Mon–Fri 1000–1445, non-match Sat 1000–1445, Sun 1000–1500; ££*) gives a two-hour tour, including a visit to the club's museum and a walk through the tunnel on to the pitch. Scottish Museum of Football (*Hampden Park; tel: (0141) 287 2746; open: Mon–Sat 1000–1700, Sun 1100–1700; ££*), expected to open during 2000, is Scotland's National Stadium and is being refurbished at a cost of £63 million. Call for information on tours and the museum.

New Lanark World Heritage Village
(See pages 154–5.)

Scotland Street School Museum
(See pages 141.)

Strathclyde Country Park

366 Hamilton Road, Motherwell. Tel: (01698) 266155.

This enormous country park has woodland trails, extensive parkland and facilities for watersports on Strathclyde Loch. There is also a theme park here, which is open daily from 1000 to 2200.

The Time Capsule

100 Buchanan Street, Coatbridge. Tel: (01236) 449572. Open: Mon–Sun 1000–2200. Extremely popular leisure centre where children can swim through primeval swamps, ride the rapids and slide down a time tunnel.

After dark

Glasgow, and of course Edinburgh, have lively annual festivals (see City Festivals, pages 36–7), when actors, dancers, singers and musicians from all over the world come to Scotland to perform. That does not mean, though, that the cities go to sleep for the rest of the year – there is always plenty to do at night.

" ... an abundant breed of men who were born to make the whole world laugh. "

Jack Webster on Glaswegians

Ballet and Opera

Scotland has its own national companies, the **Scottish Opera** and the **Scottish Ballet**, which perform in both Glasgow and Edinburgh. Productions are also frequently staged by visiting companies, including prestigious Russian troupes and sharp, contemporary dance companies.

Theatre

Theatres here stage everything from large-scale musicals such as *Les Miserables* to traditional plays and pantomimes. You can also see fresh and innovative works at Edinburgh's **Traverse Theatre**, which specialises in new writing, and at Glasgow's **Citizens' Theatre**.

Edinburgh

Church Hill Theatre
33 Morningside Road.
Tel: (0131) 447 7597.

Edinburgh Festival Theatre
13–29 Nicolson Street.
Tel: (0131) 529 6000.

Edinburgh Playhouse
18–22 Greenside Place.
Tel: (0131) 557 2590.

King's Theatre
2 Leven Street.
Tel: (0131) 529 6000.

**Royal Lyceum
Theatre Company**
Grindlay Street.
Tel: (0131) 248 4848.

Traverse Theatre
Cambridge Street.
Tel: (0131) 228 1404.

Glasgow

Centre for Contemporary Arts
270 Sauchiehall Street at McLellan
Galleries. Tel: (0141) 332 7521.

Citizens' Theatre
119 Gorbals Street.
Tel: (0141) 429 0022.

King's Theatre
256 Bath Street.
Tel: (0141) 248 5153.

**Royal Scottish Academy
of Music and Drama**
100 Renfrew Street.
Tel: (0141) 332 4101.

Theatre Royal
Hope Street. Tel: (0141) 332 3321.
The home of Scottish Opera.
The Scottish Ballet also performs
here regularly.

Tramway
25 Albert Drive.
Tel: (0141) 287 5563.

Tron Theatre
63 Trongate. Tel: (0141) 552 4267.

Glasgow is home to a
puppet theatre:

**Scottish Mask and
Puppet Theatre**
8–10 Balcarres Avenue, Kelvindale.
Tel: (0141) 339 6185.

175

Cinema

You can see everything in these two cities, from big-screen blockbusters to art-house pictures and classic black-and-white movies.

Edinburgh

ABC
120 Lothian Road.
Tel: (0131) 229 3030.

Cameo Cinema
Home Street. Tel: (0131) 228 4141.

Dominion
18 Newbattle Terrace.
Tel: (0131) 447 4771.

Drum Complex
Greenside Place. When this multi-million-pound complex opens, it should bring many film premières to Edinburgh.

Filmhouse
88 Lothian Road.
Tel: (0131) 228 2688.

Odeon Cinema
7 Clerk Street. Tel: 0870 505 0007.

UCI
Kinnaird Park. Tel: (0131) 669 0777. Multiplex cinema about 15 minutes out of the centre of town.

Glasgow

Glasgow Film Theatre
12 Rose Street. Tel: (0141) 332 6535. Independent cultural cinema

Grosvenor
Ashton Lane. Tel: (0141) 339 4298.

Odeon Cinemas
56 Renfield Street.
Tel: (0141) 332 3413.

Classical Music

Edinburgh

The Queen's Hall
89 Clerk Street. Tel: (0131) 668 2019.

Usher Hall
Lothian Road. Tel: (0131) 228 8616. Edinburgh's finest concert hall.

Glasgow

Glasgow Royal Concert Hall
2 Sauchiehall Street. Tel: (0141) 333 9123 for info or (0141) 332 6633 for tickets. Prestigious venue where you can see the Scottish Proms, as well as national and international orchestras.

Henry Wood Hall
73 Claremont Street. Tel: (0141) 225 3555. Headquarters for the Royal Scottish National Orchestra.

Other musical venues

Glasgow

Everyone loves to play Glasgow as it's always such a great atmosphere.

Scottish Exhibition and Conference Centre (SECC)
Tel: (0141) 248 3000. Not just a conference centre. Also used for concerts by major bands and stars such as Tina Turner.

The best times to see live jazz or folk music is obviously during the annual festivals staged by each city. Aside from this, plenty of pubs and bars feature live music on certain nights of the week, and there are also regular *ceilidhs*. Your best bet is to pick up a copy of *The List*, the cities' version of London's *Time Out*, which will give all the events that are going on. Also buy the evening papers – the *Evening News* in Edinburgh and the *Evening Times* in Glasgow.

Clubs

The club scene is lively in both Glasgow and Edinburgh, attracting a mix of people from students to young professionals. Both cities have thriving gay scenes. Again, you are best to consult *The List* when you get here, as things change very quickly.

Edinburgh
The Ark
3 Semple Street.
Tel: (0131) 229 7733.
The Cavendish
3 West Tollcross.
Tel: (0131) 228 3252.
CC Blooms
23–4 Greenside Place.
Tel: (0131) 556 9331.
Club Mercado
36–9 Market Street.
Tel: (0131) 226 4224.

Jazz Joint
Morrison Street.
Tel: (0131) 538 7385.
Peppermint Lounge
Blair Street. Tel: (0131) 622 8811.
Po Na Na
43b Frederick Street.
Tel: (0131) 226 2224.
Why Not?
The Dome, George Street.
Tel: (0131) 624 8633.

Glasgow
Alaska
142 Bath Lane. Tel: (0141) 248 1777.
The Apartment
23 Royal Exchange Square. Tel: (0141) 221 7808.
Babaza
Royal Exchange Square.
Tel: (0141) 204 0101.
Club Budda
142 St Vincent Street.
Tel: (0141) 221 2213.
Polo Lounge
84 Wilson Street.
Tel: (0141) 553 1221.
Reds
375 Sauchiehall Street.
Tel: (0141) 331 1635.
Sub Club
22 Jamaica Street.
Tel: (0141) 248 4600.
Yang
33 Queen Street.
Tel: (0141) 248 8484.

" If the audience at The Empire didn't like a performance, the star didn't suffer something as ordinary as boos and bad reviews; he left scarred for life. "

John Millar on The Glasgow Empire

Practical information

Practical information

Airports

Glasgow has two airports: Prestwick (*tel: (01292) 479822*), about 48km (30 miles) out of town, which links with London Stansted, Dublin, Belfast, Donegal and Paris Beauvais, and Glasgow Airport (*tel: (0141) 887 1111*), which is about 13km (8 miles) out of town. Glasgow Airport has a range of flights to and from North America, Europe and the rest of the UK.

Regular trains run from Prestwick to Glasgow Central Station – the journey takes around 45 minutes. There is also a half-hourly bus service to the city centre (the bus journey will take about one and a half hours). From Glasgow Airport buses run every 15 to 20 minutes to Buchanan Bus Station in the city centre. You can also get licensed airport taxis that wait outside.

There is a Tourist information desk at Glasgow Airport (*tel: (0141) 848 4440*).

Edinburgh Airport (*tel: (0131) 333 1000*) is about 15km (9 miles) from the city centre. Flights come in from all over Europe and the UK. There is a regular shuttle bus that runs into the city centre and takes about 25 minutes. It is considerably cheaper than taking one of the licensed airport taxis that wait outside the airport.

Tip

You are advised never to use anything other than a proper licensed taxi.

Climate

No one comes to Scotland for the weather – which is just as well! Generally Glasgow is warmer and wetter than Edinburgh, which is often blasted by icy winds from the North Sea. Edinburgh also gets the 'haar', a thick, damp sea mist that descends and can sometimes be so bad that it obscures the Forth Railway Bridge. In recent years, the winters have been

quite mild and there has been very little snow, but spring and summer have been cold and wet. The advantage of this is that, when the sun does shine, neither city gets too hot and sticky, and the air always stays fresh.

Currency

Although the unit of currency is the pound, the same as it is in England, you will notice that bank notes are generally Scottish (although English notes are legal tender). Notes are issued by the Royal Bank of Scotland, the Bank of Scotland and the Clydesdale Bank. Pound notes are also still in circulation, although more and more pound coins are appearing in your change. The pound is divided into 100 pence, and there are coins of 1, 2, 5, 10, 20, and 50 pence. Notes are 1, 5, 10, 20, 50 and 100 pounds.

There are foreign exchange services at the airports and at major branches of American Express, Thomas Cook and British Airways Travel Shops. You'll also find cash dispensers or ATMs (Automatic Teller Machines) outside major banks, and at airports and stations.

Customs regulations

Travellers coming into Scotland from outside the UK should be aware that animals should not be brought here as strict quarantine restrictions still apply, unless your pet qualifies under the Passports for Pets scheme. Check with the British embassy or consulate about specific regulations before travelling.

Electricity

The power supply in Scotland is the same as in the rest of the UK – 230/240 volts AC.

Entry formalities

EU citizens can enter Scotland with just a passport. Citizens from Australia, New Zealand, Canada, South Africa and the USA do not need a visa if they intend to stay for under 6 months. If you are coming from any other country a visa will be necessary.

Health

If you are a member of another EU country, Form E111 entitles you to free, or cheaper, medical treatment in Britain. Keep any receipts as you will need them when claiming reimbursement on Form E111 or on your insurance.

In the 1980s, Edinburgh gained an unwelcome reputation as the AIDS capital of Europe, due to the needle-sharing habits of its drug users. Sensible precautions should obviously be taken.

Information

Glasgow Tourist Information Office *11 George Square, Glasgow G2 1DY. Tel: (0141) 204 4400; fax: (0141) 221 3524; e-mail: enquiries@seeglasgow.com.*

Edinburgh and Lothian's Tourist Board *3 Princes Street, Edinburgh EH2 2QP. Tel: (0131) 473 3800; fax: (0131) 473 3849.*

Events information
Edinburgh Festival Fringe
Tel: (0131) 226 5138.

Edinburgh International Book Festival
Tel: (0131) 228 5444; programme hotline 09065 500.
Edinburgh International Festival
Tel: (0131) 473 2001.

Edinburgh International Film Festival
Tel: (0131) 228 4051.

Edinburgh International Jazz and Blues Festival *Tel: (0131) 668 2019.*

Edinburgh Military Tattoo
Tel: (0131) 225 1188; www.edintattoo.co.uk.

Websites
Information on Edinburgh
www.edinburgh.org.

Information for the whole of Britain
www.visitbritain.com.

Site for Glasgow's museums and galleries *www.glasgow.gov.uk or www.natgalscot.ac.uk.*

Site covers Glasgow Cathedral and Historic Scotland properties *www.historic-scotland.gov.uk*.

Covers National Trust for Scotland properties *www.nts.org.uk*.

Rail information
Tel: 08457 48 49 50.

Publications
The List is a fortnightly guide to what's on in Edinburgh and Glasgow and is available in newsagents. The main newspapers read in Edinburgh are *The Scotsman*, a daily broadsheet, and the *Evening News*. The main newspapers read in Glasgow are *The Herald*, a daily broadsheet and the *Evening Times*. The Sunday broadsheet newspapers are *Scotland on Sunday* and *The Sunday Herald*. You will also see the *Daily Record*, which is the main daily Scottish tabloid.

Insurance

EU citizens should travel with Form E111, which will ensure that any medical expenses are reimbursed. You are also advised to take out your own comprehensive travel insurance.

If you have a valid overseas driving licence you can use it to drive in Britain for up to one year. Visitors bringing their own licence from overseas require 'green card' insurance and should carry the registration documents for their car.

Maps

Tourist offices have free, good-quality maps of the cities available, so get hold of one as soon as you can. If you stop and look at a map in Glasgow people will almost certainly come up and ask if you're lost and need any help – they are then as likely to take you where you want to go, as give you directions.

Opening times

Shops generally open Monday to Saturday, 0900 until 1730 or 1800, and will stay open till 1900 or later on Thursdays. Many shops will also open on Sundays.

Usually banks open Monday to Friday, 0900 or 1000 until 1600 or 1700.

Post offices: main post offices are open Monday to Friday from 0900 to 1700 and on Saturday mornings. Small sub-post offices often close on Wednesday afternoon.

183

Most **museums and attractions** are open between 0900 and 1700 Monday to Saturday, and also open on Sundays. You are advised to check times before setting off if you are making a long journey.

Public holidays

Public holidays in Scotland are not always the same as in the rest of the UK – and are not even the same in Glasgow as in Edinburgh. To confuse matters further, banks may take UK holidays, but everywhere else may be open. The 2nd of January is always a holiday in Scotland. Businesses in Edinburgh may close on the first Monday in July, at the start of the traditional Trades Holiday, when factories would shut down for two weeks in July. The same applies in

Glasgow at the start of the Glasgow Fair, two weeks later. Instead of August Bank Holiday, businesses may close on a Monday in mid September.

Reading

Complicity. **Iain Banks**' novel is set in Edinburgh and has been made into a film.

Dr Jekyll and Mr Hyde. **Robert Louis Stevenson**'s famous short story about a respectable doctor, who turns into a werewolf at night, is set in London. However, it was inspired by an Edinburgh character.

Growing up in the Gorbals by Ralph Glasser and *A Glasgow Trilogy* by George Friel are fascinating accounts of life in Glasgow.

The Heart of Midlothian. **Sir Walter Scott**'s tale of old Edinburgh.

Kidnapped. Here's one for the children. **Robert Louis Stevenson**'s classic adventure story is partly set in Edinburgh.

No Mean City by A McArthur and H Kingsley Long. Published in the 1930s, this famous novel depicted life in the slums of the old Gorbals, where violence ruled.

Notes from a Small Island by Bill Bryson. In his highly amusing tour of Britain, American author **Bill Bryson** visits both Edinburgh and Glasgow. Although Bryson took his trip after many years spent living in Britain, he still found the Glasgow accent all but impenetrable.

The Prime of Miss Jean Brodie. **Dame Muriel Spark**'s novel about a prim Edinburgh schoolmistress.

The Town below the Ground. **Jan-Andrew Henderson**'s book is a factual account of the underground slum that developed under Edinburgh's Old Town. It also relates many of the ghost stories associated with this area.

Trainspotting. **Irvine Walsh**'s best-selling novel about the hidden world of the Edinburgh drug scene.

Safety and security

Both Glasgow and Edinburgh are safer than many other cities in Britain, but you should still be sensible and avoid wandering through lonely, badly lit areas at night.

In an emergency call 999 for fire, police or ambulance.

Telephones

There are plenty of public telephones in Glasgow and Edinburgh. Some will take coins – generally 10p, 20p, 50p and £1. Others require pre-paid phonecards, which you can buy in newsagents such as WHSmith.

Directory enquiries is 192, which is free from a call box.

Operator services – 100.

To make an international call dial 00 followed by the country code and then the number minus the initial zero.

Time

In winter Greenwich Mean Time (GMT) applies. In summer the clocks go forward one hour.

If you lose anything don't assume that there is no point in looking for it, as people will often hand items in to police or nearby shops. In fact if you drop a wallet or purse, there is a good chance someone will run after you to give it back.

The Police headquarters in Edinburgh is at Fettes Avenue; Strathclyde Police Headquarters is at Pitt Street.

If you lose items on a bus or train, contact the appropriate company or ask at the main bus or train station.

Tipping

In restaurants and cafés the usual tip is 10–15 per cent, and taxi drivers expect a tip too. You can also tip tour guides, porters and attendants in toilets.

Toilets

There are public toilets at the main stations. Department stores also have toilets for their customers' use, as do bars and restaurants.

Travellers with disabilities

New **buildings** have disabled access, but this
is not guaranteed with all older buildings, some
areas of which may only be reached by narrow,
winding stairs. **Black taxis** should be accessible
for wheelchairs, but **public transport** still
presents problems. The Scottish Tourist Board
has a series of symbols denoting whether
accommodation has disabled access. A
wheelchair indicates unassisted wheelchair
access; a wheelchair and attendant implies

that you will need assistance; and a person with a stick shows accessibility for visitors with mobility difficulties.

For further information contact **Lothian Coalition of Disabled People** (*tel: (0131) 475 2360*), **Free Wheel Chair Loan Service** (*tel: (0131) 469 3942*) or **Capability Scotland Advice Service** (*tel: (0131) 313 5510*).

Walking

Glasgow and Edinburgh are both great bases from which to go hill walking. Always make sure that you are properly equipped, with maps, compasses, walking boots, waterproofs, jumpers and so on, as the weather can change very suddenly. Lots of good books with suggestions for interesting walks are available – check out the local bookshops.

Index

Editorial, design and production credits

Project management: Dial House Publishing Services

Series editor: Christopher Catling

Copy editor: Lucy Thomson

Proof-readers: Lucy Thomson and Kate Owen

Series and cover design: Trickett & Webb Limited

Cover artwork: Wenham Arts

Text layout: Wenham Arts

Map work: PS Cartography

Repro and image setting: Z2 Repro, Thetford, Norfolk, UK

Printed and bound by: Artes Graficas Elkar S. Coop, Bilbao, Spain

Acknowledgements

We would like to thank Neil Setchfield for the photographs used in this book, to whom the copyright belongs, with the exception of the following:

John Heseltine: pages 149 and 161

The Still Moving Picture Co: page 150

New Lanark Conservation: page 155